"This is an important, beautiful book, and I can't imagine how American literature has gone so long without it. From as far back as West and Still right up to such contemporary poets as Hicks and Fisher, this is a collection popping at the seams with grace, preservation, sadness, joy and—most importantly—hope. *Coal: A Poetry Anthology* belongs in anyone's home who cares about good writing."
  —Silas House, author of *The Coal Tattoo* and *Clay's Quilt*

"This collection of poems promises to inspire thought and conversation about the complicated relationship between coal, society, and culture. Now, more than ever, Americans should attend to the many ways in which life and death are shaped, not only by coal, but by our appetite for energy."
  —Dr. Shaunna Scott, President Elect, Appalachian Studies Association and author of *Two Sides to Everything: The Cultural Construction of Class Consciousness in Harlan County, Kentucky*

"The book provides an outlet for residents of the central Appalachian coal region, as well as the major poets, to talk about their love and pride of their home and heritage of working in the mines. *Coal: A Poetry Anthology* supports the mission of the Mountaintop Removal writers' tours of Kentuckians for the Commonwealth and the Ohio Valley Environmental Coalition as they unite citizens from the flatlands of the cities, farms and white-water lodges with the coal-country residents in all Appalachia. A mutual effort will more effectively address the problem of stopping the destruction of our mountains and streams."
  —Mary Popham, Kentuckians for the Commonwealth

"Just as coal itself is formed from natural matter compressed and aged in a way that gives it both unity and utility, these poems are formed from material which has come out of the lives of people, aged and compressed and hardened into finished pieces which help readers understand life and death in the coalfields. Although coal is dirty and ugly, this anthology is quite the opposite because it illuminates the way that the human spirit has emerged triumphant in the face of the degradation of the land and people."
  —George Brosi, Editor, *Appalachian Heritage*

Coal
A Poetry Anthology

Chris Green

Chris Green

Oct. 2014 —
For believers
in KFTC that
helped face
down
the
Broadform
Deed.

Editor

Preface by Denise Giardina

Introduction by the Editor

Afterword by Jack Spadaro

Blair Mountain Press
Ashland, Kentucky

Blair Mountain Press
2027 Oakview Road
Ashland, Kentucky 41101

Publisher's Cataloging-in-Publication

Coal : a poetry anthology / editor, Chris Green.
    p. cm.
    Includes bibliographical references.
    LCCN 2006927507
    ISBN 0-9768817-1-3

    1. Coal mines and mining--Appalachian Region--Poetry.
    2. American poetry--Appalachian Region.
    3. Appalachian Region--Poetry.   I. Green, Chris
(Christopher A.)

    PS595.M5C63 2006   811'.0080355
                           QBI06-600252

Special thanks to Kris Clifford and Michele Schiavone
and thanks to Edwina Pendarvis
whose thoughtful and constant aid made this project possible
Cover Photograph by Victor M. Depta

This book is dedicated to the poets whose devotion
to the Appalachian mountains and people continues
to inspire:

Joseph Barrett
Carley Rees Bogarad
Muriel Miller Dressler
Lee Howard
June Jordan
Louise McNeill
Jim Wayne Miller
Brenda Morris
Bob Snyder
James Still
Jesse Stuart
Arline Thorn
Don West
James Wright

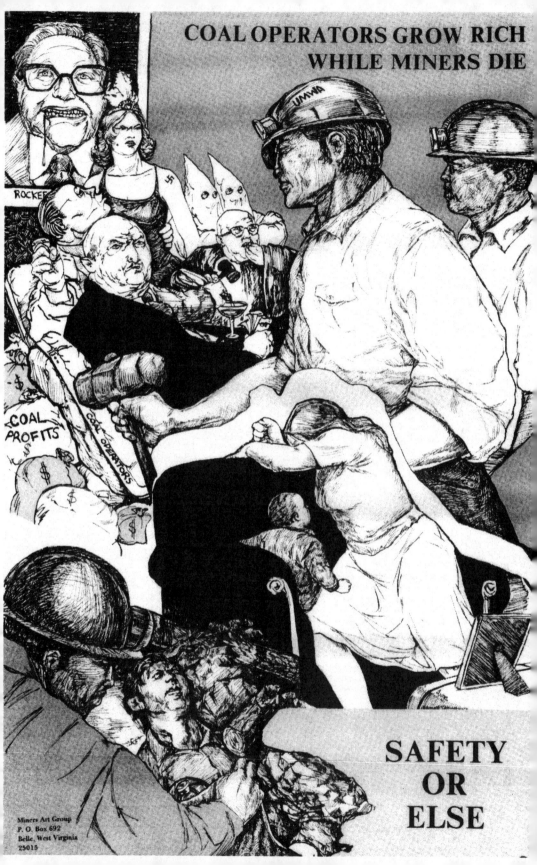

PREFACE

By Denise Giardina

When you say the word "coal," you do not think of poetry. Poems are about people—family, friends, lovers, children. Or poems are about the natural world—flowers, animals, trees, rivers, mountains. Poems are about romantic ruins, like Wordsworth's "Tintern Abbey." Or great philosophical questions, like Arnold's "Dover Beach." Or the metaphysics of John Donne or T.S. Eliot.

But "coal"? Coal is a hard, filthy, ugly rock. Its only use is utilitarian, and whatever benefits it provides of light and warmth it takes away in destruction and death.

And because coal destroys and kills, we do indeed wind our way backward as we consider it—to mountains, rivers, trees, animals, flowers, children, lovers, friends, family. Coal is a fit subject for poetry in an odd way, as Satan was a fit subject for Milton's *Paradise Lost*. Coal destroys and so it must be confronted, and what better way, what more "anti-coal" act could there be, than to write a poem?

Those unfamiliar with coal may consider it a monolithic topic for a collection of poetry. This volume gives the lie to that. The poets here are many and varied. Their work shows that "coal" is a starting point on the way to illuminating the world. It is ironic that one utilitarian function of coal is light. In these poems, the light and the power come from words.

It would be unfair to the many wonderful poets represented here to call out individuals by name. For that I will send you to the Table of Contents. I will only add that the list of those included here is wide, comprehensive and generous. Anyone who loves the poetry of place will find old friends and new in these pages, and will find as well the great Appalachian poets of the past resurrected. The poems are organized topically into six groups covering such broad subjects as miners and disasters, coal towns and families.

But the poems themselves speak, as all good poems do, to the universal. Tintern Abbey or Coal Tipple. Dover Beach or Buffalo Creek. Grecian Urn or Coal Bucket. The poet finds beauty and joy, tragedy and death, tears and inspiration in all. And to all destruction and death, whatever the source, a poem stands as the ultimate act of defiance.

Introduction

Coal & Central Appalachia

The history of mountain culture and coal in central Appalachia is not simple or short, but we would like to make a few observations.[1] First, inhabitants of the region have been closely defined by their relationship to the land, from which industries extract coal and timber (and export them for a great profit). Coal companies squeeze as much as they can out of the coalfields and their people, doing so at the cost of workers' lives, the community's health, and the health of the natural environment; unionization, regulation, and coalitions of public-interest groups have long pushed back against this squeeze. The extremes to which the coal industry will go have become all too clear: violating safety regulations, paying penalties when they must (but often not fixing the problems), polluting waterways, and lopping off mountain peaks. Apparently, the major stockholders of coal companies feel that this damage to workers, communities, and the land is acceptable, but a growing number of people disagree.

Due to growing industrialization and the expansion of railroads into the region, the countryside of central Appalachia was transformed in the decades following 1880. From a hardwood forest dotted with farms and small towns, coal camps sprang up by the dozens, and for the next sixty years, these camps echoed with energy: passenger trains rumbled up to the station to pick up and drop off passengers; coal trains stopped below the tipple with coal rolling down the chute into the cars; water tanks gushed water over the coal to clean it and wet it down; and everywhere rang the voices of miners, their wives, and children. The first sixty years were times of great pros-

---

[1] Because we lack room to expand upon this history, we have included a brief bibliography at the end of the book to provide a wider context for the poems herein.

perity and conflict. As billions of tons of coal flowed from the mountains and hundreds of men lost their lives each year, the miners and the UMWA fought for safety regulations, health care, fair hours, and fair pay.

Central Appalachian coal fields were not easily unionized, however, as the West Virginia mine wars, the Battle of Blair Mountain, and Bloody Harlan demonstrated. But over the years, miners gained income, rights, and respect. After a series of booms and busts and mechanization of the mines, however, the coal camps were shut down. Towns like Welch, West Virginia, and Jenkins, Kentucky, have managed to hang onto only a small percentage of the population they had when the coal business boomed. Today, of course, the industry has changed: while deep mines offer good pay for the few miners who remain, the work is still hazardous. Surface mining is safer, but in addition to the decimation of the labor force, its ugly effects are clear—reverberations of blasts crack the foundations and walls of homes and other buildings, toxic chemicals turn streams black, and the "overburden" (layers of the mountain between the surface and the coal) from mountaintop mining buries hundreds of miles of streams.

Over the last 130 years, the land and people of central Appalachia have been defined in part by the struggles of others to wrest the wealth from under their feet. For good and ill, people in central Appalachia have incorporated their relationships with the coal industry into their cultures, including the connection to place, the great loss of land rights, the influx of immigrants, the exodus of natives to find work elsewhere, and the grandchildren who remain and reveal with reverence the miners' hats with carbide lamps that their grandfathers wore. The melding of coal and culture also shows how people who work with coal take pride in their jobs, both the daily, hard work of mining *and* the work of fighting for their rights. On a national level, one of the most important stories in labor history is how the unionization of the coalfields established essential rights and laws for all working people. However, the last half-century has seen a tremendous reduction in the number of coal workers and the reduction of unions while *at the same time* coal production has increased and profits for companies are higher than ever. It is no surprise that those counties producing the most coal in central Appalachia also have the highest poverty and infant mortality rates in the nation. Culture in central Appalachia has come to be defined by what both was (and is) destroying it, even as coal gives people work from which they have rightly taken self-definition. This combination of work, lost land, pride, and suffering is at the core of the contradictions that animate the region's culture and the poems in this anthology.

January 2006 initiated a year of tragedy in the coal mines of West Virginia and eastern Kentucky; only one of the miners trapped in the Sago mine came out alive. That disaster became a focal point for renewed efforts to make mining safer. Both tragedy and hope have a long history in the hills of the Appalachian coalfields, and the outcome of this new round of attention to the human costs of mining is uncertain. Poems in this collection recount personal connections to the recent disasters like Sago and Aracoma, to past tragedies like the 1972 Buffalo Creek flood, and to potential tragedies like the threat hanging over Marsh Fork Elementary School, where children study in classrooms and play on a playground less than 300 feet away from a coal preparation plant and impoundment dam storing 2.8 billion gallons of toxic slurry. A spill from the same type of slurry ruined seventy miles of waterways and damaged hundreds of lives when an impoundment dam broke in Martin County, Kentucky, a few years ago, unleashing 250 million gallons of sludge—an environmental tragedy that dwarfs the Exxon Valdez, which unleashed 11 million gallons.

The nature of the poems we received made it especially ironic to read a recent article in *The Chronicle of Higher Education* that referred to poor people in West Virginia as "human slag." The author blamed the coal industry for the supposed ruination of people in the coalfields but seemed ignorant of the complexities underlying coal companies' crimes. In particular, the writer (an academic and documentarian) seemed unaware of the contradictory role played by academics and image makers in the exploitative relationship between industries and their workers. We hope not to make the same mistake. We recognize that academics live in comparative comfort partly because of the exploitation of coal miners and that any book we publish stands to participate in that exploitation. We hope, though, that the collection does more good than harm by providing a public forum for the perspectives of poets, all of whom, like us, love this place and its cultures—and many of whom live much closer to the reality of coal mining than we do.

Though we conceived this book as focusing on the experiences of people in central Appalachia, we are well aware that the costs of coal are not just in mining and are not just local. The coal fuels electrical generation plants all over the nation: the electricity for light you will be turning on tonight was likely generated by the people the poems portray. As consumers of electricity, almost every person and industry in the United States (and millions outside of our borders) are directly involved. The air pollution caused by coal-burning electrical generators has terrible effects on people, animals, and vegetation throughout the United States and the world beyond. The recent mine disasters brought national and international attention to the terrible dangers the industry represents for miners, but that attention did not result in efforts to address the more widespread dangers that the industry poses for everyone.

The Anthology

An anthology makes an implicit claim of adequately representing the topic, group, or period represented in it. To clarify and qualify our claim, we want to share the process of how we put the book together (because we know that we have overlooked poems that might be here) and explain the rationale behind our layout and design.

As we discussed building this anthology, we were amazed to discover that no such poetry anthology existed for the region of central Appalachia.[2] We first announced a call for poems about coal mining and its effects on miners, families, communities, and the environment. We decided to focus on the bituminous coal fields of central Appalachia (West Virginia, eastern Kentucky, western Virginia, and southern Ohio) because, although many differences exist between cultures in the region, differences would have expanded exponentially if we also included Pennsylvania, western Kentucky, southern Indiana, Illinois, or the coal fields in the west. We have, however, chosen to include a few poems by poets who write about coal fields outside of central Appalachia because we felt those poems spoke to our region's culture and history. In response to our call, over 300 poems were submitted, some 80 of which are in this volume.

In selecting poems we sought to present a range of experience, voice, and style—a range, in other words, of aesthetics, audience, and purpose. We knew that the poetry we were receiving was part of a tradition and history, which it also became our mission to represent. The poetry of coal in central Appalachia has been composed since Don West first began writing when he was organizing with the National Miners Union in Bell and Harlan counties, Kentucky, in the mid-1930s. As a result, we looked at thousands of poems from books and journals, and we selected another 70 or so to include.[3] To ensure appreciation of the poems' great variety, we have noted, at the end of each poem, where and when the poem (if published before) was published. Brief author biographies are found at the end of the book. We encourage you to consider who wrote the poems as well as where and when they were published. We think you will be pleasantly surprised at the variety of presses and social justice movements that have been a regular presence in central Appalachia for many years.

---

[2] For an excellent anthology on coal mining in Pennsylvania see *Coalseam: Poems from the Anthracite Region*, Karen Blomain, ed. Scranton: University of Scranton Press, 1996.

We must warn you that we have not made an all-out effort to be inclusive; we decided the work of some poets was already being done by others that we (to be honest) preferred. Regardless, some of the poems we have assembled are raw in style and voice: they are not all finished products written by practiced poets for a literary journal. Nevertheless, all poems included are written by people honoring the complexities, despairs, and richness of coal and culture in the mountains. We are pleased with the scope and depth of experience herein.

While it is a poem's nature to break, thwart, and operate outside of boundaries, *Coal* is broken into six sections, each of which houses poems gathered around a particular viewpoint: (1) Miners & Work, (2) Disasters & Mining, (3) Family & Community, (4) Life after the Mines, (5) Environmental Degradation, and (6) Resistance. These sections are not mutually exclusive, and often poems in one section might have been placed in another, but we hope that grouping the poems will invite readers to think about the relationship of different perspectives.

We have also (for the most part) arranged the poems in each section chronologically according to the subject portrayed. If you will, consider reading this anthology as analogous to watching the place where a river enters an estuary. One way to learn about the landscape the river flowed through would be to collect leaves (and, unfortunately, plastic...) from it. The order in which you found the leaves would tell you much about the river. In the same way, these poems might be thought of as floating on rivers of history and culture. The poems, al- though not fully revealing that history and culture, point the way. By following the flow of the poems, you may perhaps better discern the story of the landscapes that have brought these poems to you.

---

[3] For a list of the poems that we found in four important anthologies, see the bibliography.

CONTENTS

II Disasters & Mining

III Families & Community

V Environmental Degradation

VI Resistance

I

Miners & Work

Earth-Bread

Under stars cool as the copperhead's eyes,
Under hill-horizons cut clean and deft with wind,
Beneath this surface night, below earth and rock,
The picks strike into veins of coal, oily and rich
And centuries-damp.

They dig with short heavy strokes, straining shoulders
Practiced and bulging with labor,
Crumbling the marrow between the shelving slate,
Breaking the hard, slow-yielding seams.
Bent into flesh-knots the miners dig this earth-bread,
This stone-meat, these fruited bones.

This is the eight-hour death, the daily burial
In a dark harvest lost as any dead.

James Still

(*Hounds on the Mountain*, Viking, 1937)

Poets of Darkness

Make them poets of the darkness,
For they speak from black faces
Lapping the sounds like red tongued dogs
Hurried after water.
We have seen them
Hunkered in the guts of steel
And we have seen their mantrips of segmented rusting cars
Being sucked and swallowed by long black holes.

Yes, make them poets
Make them hands of fossil ferns,
Give them grips on black diamond pens,
Have them speak Paleozoic languages
Decoded from Rosettas made of coal.

Make them tell us
What it means to see into aeons
Where no man has seen.

James B. Goode

(*Up from the Mines*, Jesse Stuart Foundation, 1993)

Miners wanted:

>dig coal
>under miles
>of mountain;
>learn about buggies,
>loaders, boons,
>blasting caps,
>timbers, dummies,
>tamping rods;
>pray
>destroy wall
>without
>collapsing ceiling.

Conditions:
>dank darkness;
>56 degrees;
>ceilings of dripping,
>dripping rock;
>crawl, stoop,
>breathe rock
>dust, coal dust,
>sulfur, carbide fumes;
>noxious gases
>soak to skin.

Skills required:
>must stay sharp
>for cut-throughs
>to poisonous air pockets
>or walls of rushing,
>putrid water;
>petrified tree
>stumps overhead—

"Kettle bottoms,"
"Widow makers";
sudden loss of oxygen—
"Black damp";
and every day—
"Fire in the hole!"
Benefits:
$15 a day;
black lung.

Apply inside.

Delilah F. O'Haynes

(*The Character of Mountains*, Appalachian
Authors Guild, 2006)

Miner Shaking Hands with a Union Man

from a photograph

These men are solemn and strong,
their lungs black and bituminous.
Behind the photographer, Peabody's goons.

The woman, half-visible on the fringe
of the vignette, feels that way:
her husband vanished in the dark snow of a cave in.

And closely, through the heavy grain,
you can see they are armed.
The blunt handle of a shovel curled

in an arm's crook, a chain
wrapped around a fist
like a large and fraternal ring.

This is a show of force: it is not
important that the pale-skinned Peabody men
sweat around the butts of revolvers,

but that they know for once
the isolation of the mines,
the impenetrable blackness off camera.

Robert Wrigley

(*The Sinking of Clay City*, Copper Canyon Press, 1979)

Night in the Coal Camps

Cold yellow windows to the night, the trees
Frozen with dark, and eyes sleepless
Along rutted streets. Clear the sparrow words
Pierce thumb-latched doors; blowing they pass
Like field larks dustily through seeding grass.

Drawn faces on pillows, mouths hollowed in breathing
The unquiet air; and the million-tongued night tremulous
With crickets' rasping thighs, with sharp cluckings
Of fowls under drafty floors. In the caverns deep
The picks strike into coal and slate. They do not sleep.

James Still

(*Hounds on the Mountain*, Viking, 1937)

Alva's Life

He sipped his black coffee from a bowl
        And took a bite of the raw onion, like an apple.
He strummed his worn Gibson guitar.
        And the high nasal-tone of "I'll Fly Away"
Transported him back to the hills,
Where he fished the Tug River in the moist summer nights,
Where he hunted rabbits, squirrels, and groundhogs
        To feed Emma and his five children,
Where he rose each day before dawn to work in the mine,
Where his first born, twins, died before they were two.
They buried them at the family gravesite
        On the side of the mountain at the end of the holler,
Where the family gathered for reunions
        And listened to preachers for hours,
One after another, on sin and salvation,
While the children chased each other around
        The tombstones of their ancestors,
And the sinners sat at tables eating fried chicken
        And smoking hand-rolled cigarettes.

The northern city promised a better life.
On his days off he found the wild,
Where he camped and fished on the Scioto's banks,
Where he dug night crawlers for extra money
        And stored them in a refrigerator on the back porch,
Where he raised vegetables inside the chain-linked yard
        Of his aluminum-sided ranch house.

The doctors at the VA hospital couldn't say
If it was the coal dust or the asbestos from the brake factory
        That finally did him in.
The hill people came up to his funeral
        Dressed in bib overalls and dirty boots.
Beside the coffin was his picture,
        In uniform, young and crisp and serious,

Before he got his leg shot at Normandy,
But he never once mentioned the war.
The grandson sang "I'll Fly Away"
    And carried him to the final spot,
Where a dash,
Between two dates on a simple marker,
    In a treeless cemetery with dirt lanes,
    Surrounded by gravel pits and vacant industrial lots,
Diminishes the span between birth and death.

Stephen Spencer

(*The Journal of Kentucky Studies*, 2005)

Noah Totten

all his years smoked with the haze of coal dust
   his broken father whose sad harmonica voice
      struck haunted chords in his sleep
a mother who died slowly; her small boned hands
   wrenching the pain daily from her breast
from childhood he dug into the black wombs of the mines
   his days smelled always of carbide and black water
      never enough women's arms to shelter him
   from the crash of shaky roofs over his head
   never enough whiskey to wash down the acrid taste of coal
he kept in a warped desk drawer the ancient toy pistol
      of the blond perfect son;
once he came home young swinging his lunch pail
but the look on his wife's face through the dirty pane
      made the pail stop in mid air
one fragile daughter was shattered by rheumatic fever
     those who survived made his heart hollow
      over the year with their griefs;
     but he held his spine scotch gentry straight
as he had in the terrorized days of union battles
   he grew to resemble a rocky cliff
   where the sun seldom broke out
an old man who stalked barren fields in winter
   looking for the wasted fruits
   and i know he did not lie corset stiff
   and funeral home painted inside that
      alien ruffled bed
   because i watched him slip up the far hill
   the brown flannel of his hunting shirt
   riding the path to the top of the mountain
     where he waits for me.

Mary Joan Coleman

(*Take One Blood Red Rose*, West End, 1978)

Devils Den

(1)

The shaft was cool and the darkness hides the way
A man can feel the chill in the air as he goes in
Daddy once said "A hole can smell the fear of a man
He must be brave to travel into the valley of darkness"

The reporters were waiting just outside for the story
Just beyond the marked off line Jennie Hatfield yelled
"Did any those miners die,
Tell us Big John what happened?"
Daddy just walked on slowly not even looking at the reporter

His face was colored black from the coal dust
Two white streams just below his eyes
Daddy walked toward home

(2)

I woke just before dawn
To the sound of my daddy crying
My heart was pounding
I jumped to run into his room

Mama met me at the door
I asked her "why is daddy crying"
She replied "he'll be ok
Just go back to bed"

But I hid beside the dresser
Just by the door
I was scared for my daddy
Because I never seen my daddy cry

Then I heard him whisper
"The ride was slow and dusky
And the dampness seem kinda thick
Eddie Varney was out front

The darkness covered his face, but
His voice was loud and clear
'Mag is going to have a baby,

I'm going to be a daddy'
That was the last words I heard old Eddie say

The roof rumbled like thunder
I looked for Eddie
But it was too late
The rock had buried him"

(3)

Jennie Hatfield did the cover story,
The picture on the cover was daddy carrying Eddie's casket

The Devils Den Claims Another Victim
The Sandy Mountain Chronicle
June 7, 1973

Margie Moore Wright

No Breast Augers in Heaven

(For Debra, who told me this story)

A big slate rock
Fell on Daddy's leg—
Pinned it to the muddy bottom
Like a bug on a board. . .
Squeezed it until
The life run out
In a tiny red river to the gob
And pooled up on a puddle of hydraulic oil.
He tugged, yanked, and pulled—
Finally unzipped his pants
And slid out
Bringing a gushing, mangled stub. . .
Then crawled
On all fours
Like a three legged dog
To his buddy's place
Where he passed out.
Next day
He died
On a soaked feather tick.
The breath hadn't much more
Rattled from his blackened lips,
When the bosses came
To claim the company's tools
(Even took grand daddy's carpenter tools)—
Said Daddy wouldn't have no use
For a breast auger in heaven.
"Thank God! By God,"
I said.

James B. Goode

(Appalachian Heritage, Winter 2005)

In the Mines, September 12, 1975

I never worked the coal.
Never had a friend
Die in the mines.

I only knew
His elaborate Presley-swirling hair
Breathitt County swarthy man's face
the times his face was pink and pale.
I never knew him with black Jolson face,
oceans of white
drowning his
animal seeing irises.
He never said to me:
"If you don't wanna work
 git to the house."
I only heard him say:
"Get this man a beer, what kind
 do you want, Jim?" in
the Silver Dollar
those nights when he had to
escape
Louise, the aching muscles,
the days beginning and
ending gray,
the black, gaping hole.

I helped him move once to
one of the four houses
they had
while I knew him.
Always moving, swirling
round that sucking hole,
lodging like a clorox bottle

on a creek bank
till the next heavy rain.
Always swirling, driven to that hole
      "Where it's dark as a dungeon
       and damp as the dew,
        Where the danger is double
        and the pleasures are few"
Swirl no more, Tam. Swirl no more.
Rest easy, rest easy
in that black angry hole.

Rest easy
in that black sucking hole.

              Jim Webb

Poem for Jim Trammel

May, 1976

On the bank of the Kanawha River,
with the Banks of Charleston at my back,
I watched the dark swallows
wheel over the water
until they were shadows,
until they were nothing.
A mile downstream
a barge's lean blue light
cut the watercrests.
So I crossed the bridge.

I found you under the steps,
wondering with me:
When the hell will this place open up?

Because,
in Charleston, West Virginia,
the station doesn't open up til midnight.
And the Cincinnati train doesn't leave till three.

They'd taken out all the benches
so we sat on the quarrystone stoop
and traded stories
while the highway shuddered over us:
  Your father marched with Mother Jones
  The night before Blair Mountain
  She slept in your house.
  You were one year old.

For four hours we drank good whiskey in the cold
And every hour the trains exploded past us:
  coal car coal car coal car coal car

They obliterated the mandolin.
They obliterated your stories.
They even covered up your cough.

You don't have Black Lung, Jim Trammel.
The doctor said so.
You coughed until the plastic
they put in for your stomach buckled
and you spit good whiskey out onto the stone.
But you don't have Black Lung.

You were going to Chicago,
so they made us take separate cars.
But all that rattling night long,
past the night shifts and the sleeping farms,
your red cough shook the rails.

Michael Henson

(*Mucked*, edited by Bob Henry Baber and Jim Webb,
Hesperus Press, 1978)

Shapes

When he saw people flowing out of the mountains,
leaving like a line of clanking coal cars,
his life grew damp and heavy in his flesh,
turned dark and cold
as charred wood in a rained-out fire.

The smallest thing, though, still could fire his spirit—
a chopping ax far off in the woods,
foxhounds running on the ridge at night,
the cries of children playing in the creek,
a dog lapping water in the dark.

When he found deer tracks on the logging roads
his life grew light and dry.
Near the weathered silver of old barns
his life caught fire
and he studied shapes in the flame of his own spirit.

Jim Wayne Miller

(*The Mountains Have Come Closer*, Appalachian
Consortium, 1980)

Miners

Soot-stained, like chimney sweepers,
They work underground in a wet-earthed night bed,
Where the rafters creak and lanterns dangle
On cables stretched five miles.
Large-armed, with his hard-chested wheeze,
Big bulging muscles, his hand in a torn sleeve,
The iron-lunged tunnel man with lamp hat, cinder grin.
Vainest of laborers who dig for gems in the ink light,
A miner walks the evening twice,
Moves down the sinking shafts
Like a dead weight to the dungeons of his day,
Intricate as sleep, twice as dark.

Mark Anderson

(*Wild Sweet Notes II*, edited by Ace Boggess,
Publishers Place, 2000)

The Coal Poets

I

At the mighty supermarket
where telephone poles migrate
across the street, stopping traffic,
an old coal poet leans on his cane
the body of a wheezing skeleton
jaw full of tobacco, watching
the doors swing open for
            grocery carts.
He lived with his mouth shut
with his wife who ran the kitchen,
and survived with a few buddies
drinking beer by the river,
tossing in a line at night.

What remains has more power per man
than would have been believed when
he shot it straight off the block,
            "bumpin' the solid,"
or drove a blacksmith-sharpened auger
into sulphur balls that would wrap
a man around his own hands.
            He remembers
the fraud of a swagbellied car,
the camps fenced in, the guard gates
            and the passes:
"The curfew whistle blew at nine."
"They would beat you up if you left
the lid off your garbage can."

II

Here and here
a shopping mall imitation
hatched from a spore
that settled in the wake
        of the interstate,
and displaced people from the last war
opening hallelujah chinese restaurants.
At the fast food franchise
overweight sparrows check the pickings
around a four-wheel drive special
with spray paint decals of wild geese
        in flight.
New and unused coal poets gather
to watch the terry cloth quiver:
"I ain't seen a pair like that
for a while. Them's great conductors."
"Bet that's the only thing he learned
in the eighty-hour course."
"Hey is it true that junk food
makes you a better conductor?"
"Listen, Consol's got it all, right.
Well, I went up 'ere and the sign said
for all applicants to go in the back door.
Now what's 'at tell you right off?"
"Then you go in and wait
and the secretaries start bossin
        you around."
"Don't you know, that's how they teach
you red-caps the chain of command."

P.J. Laska

(*Wages and Dreams*, 1980)

Woman and the Underground Brotherhood

I've had some good times,
think I've done the job, done it really well.
The problem wasn't work.
My biggest problem was height (four feet eleven).
Because I can carry about anything the guys can carry,
run most any of the equipment or do anything.
And I get along real good with them.

For a long time I was the only woman they'd let run the equipment.
You have to prove you can handle it,
that you're not going to cry if you mash a finger
or get a little dirt on you.

At first they didn't like the idea of us women being in there,
but one crew I worked on, a couple of them came to me one night,
told me they were glad I was there.

One day I was cleaning the dinner hole
and this big timber was in my way—I mean *it was big*—
so I just picked up one end and slung it out of the way.

The boss told the guys, "Brenda picked that up.
After she left, I tried to pick it up too, and I couldn't."
I'm 38 now, and I've lost some of my strength.
When I was younger, I could pick up a refrigerator.
I was in that kind of shape.

When we were kids, we didn't have water in the house,
had a well back up the hill and I'd carry water for Mom,
a washtub full at a time instead of a couple of buckets.

The guys, after they get to know you, tell you about their kids
and their wives and how they met and what they're getting her
for her birthday. I wouldn't trade that for anything.
Some of them aren't worth a dern,
but most of them are.

At Christmas I cooked dinner for the crew,
had the dinner hole fixed up nice for them,
tablecloth, Christmas stockings hung, a tape player,
and we had Christmas dinner.
One Christmas they took up a collection, brought me a camera.
It tickled me to death.

Once we were working section Eight South.
It was dinnertime, everybody laying down, and Bill says,
"Give me that cushion."
I said, "No, you can't have my cushion."
He says, "Well, won't you let me lay my head in your lap?"
I was the only woman down there among seven or eight.
So I said, "Okay, Bill, I'll let you lay your head in my lap,
but you gotta lay *face down*."
He hasn't spoken to me since.
I humiliated him in front of all those men.

We got this one guy aggravates me *to death* all the time.
One night he put his hand down on top my head,
pushed so hard I dropped to the ground.
I throwed my hands out to catch myself,
so he stepped on my hands, just goofing off, you know.
He's not doing it to hurt me.
The minute he lets me go of me he knows he's in for it.
I come straight off the ground against him,
shove him plum back against the wall, get a neck hold on him,
and he tries to get away so we're both rolling on the ground.
One minute I got him down, the next he's got me.

When we get up our hands are scratched all to pieces.
It's just goofing off.
The boss said, "Them guys know not to touch you.
You'll beat the shit out of them."
Some of the married guys, they'll want to go out with you,
sit there, tell you all the problems they have with their wives.
They'll act like it's their wives' fault.
At work they'll sit around and talk about women all night long,
how many they went out with over the weekend, how easy they was.
After a while you get sick of listening to stuff like that.
To them you're the same thing.
I don't pay much attention because if I did
I'd probably chop a few heads off.
I try to keep it all a joke.

After a while you don't feel like the person you were.
I think it caused a lot of problems between me and Wesley.
Rumors went around: I was sleeping with this one and that one,
going out with the bosses,
and he got to the point where everybody was telling him this stuff
and he didn't want to take my word for it
and I got tired of arguing with him:
"If you want to believe it, believe it.
If you don't, don't."

I tried going out after the divorce,
but nobody wants you as a person.
I guess I've lost a lot of my trust in men.
If they say anything I pass it off as a joke.
I told them I wasn't anything they'd want to take home to their mothers.
They call me a lady,
and I say, "Ugh!
You don't know anything about me."

It didn't bother me at first as much as it does now.
The guys call me one of the guys, and I am rough.

Basically, I've got bad manners just like one of them.
I don't care if I never dress up,
and I don't wear much jewelry or anything.
Sometimes I think, "Well, what in the world am I doing here?
I should be at home taking care of the house,
taking care of my daughter, acting like other women do."
I tried to be like nice women,
going to parties, baby showers,
but when they start playing all these little ignorant games,
it just drives me up the wall.

Sometimes I'd like to get out and quit,
but what in the world would I do?
I've got so used to being in there, working with those guys.
When I was sick and off-work for two or three days,
one of the guys came by, brought me one rose.
And they're always doing something for you.
I guess it's just what you get used to.

Brenda L. Morris and Mike Yarrow

(In the late 1970s, Ms. Morris was interviewed by Yarrow who transcribed parts of the interview into this "found" poem.)

(*Appalachian Journal*, Winter 1988)

Retired Miners

in Dr. Capelletti's office,
crippled and wheezing:

"if any guy   tells you
he got rich   through hard work
ask him   whose?"

Ed Ochester

(*Miracle Mile*, Carnegie Mellon University
Press, 1984)

My Father's Black Lungs

Rage, rage against the dying of the light.
Dylan Thomas

I

The Mingo blast furnaces
hell-fire reflections on the Ohio,
starless nights, lights in the air
like a luminous New York skyline—
seventy years of smoke and graphite
have eaten his lungs,
or is it the despair
and boredom of the unemployed
that flatten him in a bedroom
soaked in shadow?
I wish him good fortune
before he dies—
a lottery ticket for a million
dollars, a patented invention,
the attention of an important
someone, for love is not enough.

II

Everyday
he maps the ocean
floor, taking pebbles
from his pocket
to mark the site
of sunken ships
and treasures.

He stoops and
measures all his
wealth in dreams
which the current
sweeps away.

III

Somewhere he lost it:
the red center
which contains
the control switch.
Off, on—off, on,
all day he cries
over pains in his eyes.
Real blindness covers
imagined blindness
better than glasses
or a new lens made
for fingertips.
—He lost it:
the god-wad center
that holds the edge
against the knife
that slices dreams
in two like a guillotine
hitting a small fruit;
pear-drop soft, it
explodes in a basket.

IV

On the other end
of the line, black
worm for voices,
he speaks in a slur.

Slow words pity
his hardened lungs.
"Candles eat oxygen."
He has nothing else
to say. Sick Narcissus,
he swallows pills with water,
still fascinated only by
his own reflection.
Doctors prescribe
remedies, twenty capsules
a day for pain,
anxiety and sleep—
numbing the brain
as snow blankets
the jagged mountain.
A bed with headboard
filled with bottles
of tranquilizers—
black and green
screens against feeling,
and no one knows that
he is drowning
in the mirror.

V

Time has touched his face
like the autumn breeze
shaking the last
full trees.
The wind reaps
the seed he planted,
leaving a harvest
of barren ground.

VI

Like a child with croup
he sucks the air.
I stand there
against the wall
of the darkened hallway
and listen to each breath,
loving him, wishing that
he understood what went wrong
or even what went right
as he slips easy,
all too easy,
into that good night.

Carley Rees Bogarad

(*Old Wounds, New Words*, edited by Bob Henry Baber,
George Ella Lyon and Gurney Norman, Jesse Stuart
Foundation, 1994)

Unemployed Coal Miner

What
else
to
do
with
hands
except
to
put
them
into
pockets
where
nothing
is?

James Still

(*Kentucky Poetry Review*, Spring/Summer 1985)

Ain't No Pie Jobs

Another motor down
3 left has 2 inch water
cold water seeps into leaky boots
feet stay cold and ache
way past dinner
and finishing up in the shop

Hands swell from concrete too
can't wear a wedding band
even on weekends off
The grinder
manicures some nails twice
The torch burns eyes bright red
spews hot metal through two shirts

Read the bulletin board at quittin' time
maybe another job up for bid
somebody's got 9 Beagle puppies
school's all day on the 25th
good bass boat for sale
probably Lonnie's
he never got called back

No jobs posted
could be a lot worse

Remember 83?
NO WORK 'TIL FURTHER NOTICE
Thinking on the way home
of hot suppers and warm kids
trying to keep it that way.

Jenny Galloway

(*Now & Then Magazine*, Spring 1988)

The Former Miner Returns from
His First Day as a Service Worker

(at McDonald's—somewhere in Appalachia)

All day he crushed the spongy buns, pawed at
The lids of burger boxes and kiddie pacs
As if they were Chinese puzzles.

All day his hands ticked, ready to latch on
Or heave or curl around a tool
Heavier than a spatula.

All day he rubbed his eyes in the crisp light.
All day the blue tile, the polished chrome, said
Be nimble, be jolly, be quick.

All day he grinned while the public, with bland
Or befuddled faces, scowled over his head
And mumbled, whispered, snarled and snapped.

All day his co-workers, pink and scrubbed,
Prattled and glided and skipped while he,
All bulk and balk, rumbled and banged.

Near shift's end he daydreamed—of the clang
Of rock on steel, the skreel
Of a conveyor belt, the rattling whine
Of the man trip, the miner's growl of gears
As it gnarled, toothing at the seam.

He makes his slow way home, shadow among
Roadside shadows, groping back in himself
For that deep sheltering dark.
He has never been so tired.
His hands have never been so clean.

Mark DeFoe

(*Southern Humanities Review*, Winter 1988)

Thomas Mason Kelley

Thomas Mason Kelley in a Moment of Preparation

Boots By The Door
(One toe on the other, laces tangled and hard
Yesterday's dust has turned in on itself
Kick and stomp on your way through the yard
Then scrape with a flathead from the dashboard shelf)

Belt And Battery
(Juiced up from the outlet in the kitchen wall
Electrically angular, plastically black
Not unlike the rock you're paid to haul
Made to hang low in the small of your back)

Lunch In A Bucket
(Not what you'd expect in the age of the Igloo
When they pound and vacuumseal the lid down tight
For a joke, you chuck sandwich and bucket too
And grin dirty through a ten-hour appetite)

Jeans FlannelShirt HardHat LittleDebbie
CashForSmallWagers (three ones and a five)
CaseKnife JerseyGloves MarlboroLights
IdeasForThinking MerleTapesForThe Drive

Thomas Mason Kelley in a Moment of Cleanliness

Dear old Dad's dirt is all gone down the drain
And now mine, from creases deep in the neck
And from wristdirt that's crawled up into the cuff

Fine black powder on white Ivory suds
The Yin and Yang of the Coming Home
Soapy and smooth meets grainy and rough

But still I scrub, I rake the skin
   For the feel of the threads of the Wal-Mart cloth
   And that's enough

Laura Ann Kelley in a Moment of Subsistence

If he can't see that the meat's on the pan
If he can't see the fat hitting the oven coil
If he can't see the bubble when the blade cuts the can
If he can't see the potatoes boil
If he can't see the blood when the knife goes in
If he can't see the grooves on the cutting board
If he can't see the peelings on my forearmskin
If he can't see the tangle in the mixer cord

it's just the angle he looks from it's just the angle
because he sees some things sometimes when he looks and
sometimes he looks and sometimes he looks he really does

Thomas Mason Kelley in a Moment of Unrest

I've stayed quiet through it all: the LBJ forehead
and the whole Nixon scene, the Fordcarter pages
and the Ronreagan screen, and the lightshow since,
but I've kept my seat and focused in large
part on cornchips and meat, and years have been
paid for, and milkjugs and bread, and cornflakes
and gasoline deprived of its lead, until it all
tangles up in a coalblack ball, and I wonder
if I'm gonna stay quiet through it all.

Thomas Mason Kelley in a Moment of Repose

Finally time to say.
After four mines, two wives and three apples of my eye,
After a stacked spine's worth of anthracite twinges,
I'm laid off today.

Was this my last mine?
Can't say, given the rock (hard as it is) and the coal
(Not even a purpose anymore). They could call me back
And that would be fine.

Or maybe no.
Anymore, I greet topside light as I greet lawyer-letters:
On the one hand, sun on the creekrocks; on the other,
All this shit I owe.

But who's kidding who?
I've waited for this day. Not to rest but to pause,
To contemplate the toolshed, to observe myself
The way surface people do.

All this is what I see:
A walked-across yard. A screenporch where I sit
Waiting to get up and leave it. And I see regret,
But regret don't see me.

John F. Keener

(*Appalachian Journal*, Spring 1999)

Twilight in West Virginia:
Six O'Clock Mine Report

Bergoo Mine No. 3 will work: Bergoo Mine
No. 3 will work tomorrow. Consol. No. 2
will not work: Consol. No. 2 will not
work tomorrow.

Green soaks into the dark trees.
The hills go clumped and heavy
over the foxfire veins
at Clinchfield, One-Go, Greenbrier.

At Hardtack and Amity the grit
abrades the skin. The air is thick
above the black leaves, the open mouth
of the shaft. A man with a burning

carbide lamp on his forehead
swings a pick in a narrow corridor
beneath the earth. His eyes flare
white like a horse's, his teeth glint.

From his sleeves of coal, fingers
with black half-moons: he leans
into the tipple, over the coke oven
staining the air red, over the glow

from the rows of fiery eyes at Swago.
Above Slipjohn a six-ton lumbers down
the grade, its windows curtained with soot.
No one is driving.

The roads get lost in the clotted hills,
in the Blue Spruce maze, the red cough,
the Allegheny marl, the sulphur ooze.

The hill-cuts drain; the roads get lost
and drop at the edge of the strip job.
The fires in the mines do not stop burning.

Irene McKinney

(*Six O'Clock Mine Report*, University of
Pittsburgh Press, 1989)

Overtime

"Don't work another hoot owl," she begs
I just force the phone back into its cradle.
The slate colored sky is sinkin' behind the hill.
Travis has his first game in two weeks,
And I'll be damned if he doesn't get a new uniform.

There's a man-trip down at 19-23 switch
And if I don't show those red-hats how to fix it
They might wind up killin' me one day.
They don't know their asses from—
Better hang up my check-tag before I head under.
It's that or a $250 fine.

I rub its round, brassy surface with "Persinger"
And my social security number on it.
It's my lucky tag, I tell myself,
Not a message that I'm trapped or crushed
In the belly of this black hill.

I grip tight my thermos,
Knowing it's fulla hot coffee from home
I know Judy worries, but she's gonna smile
When I buy her that new car in a month or so.
She's had nice ones, but they've all been used.

I drop, like sky into darkness
In this creaky elevator.
Kenny knows I've worked double
About four times this month.
I won't crawl on my knees for the rest of my life.

Jenny Adams

Section Boss

He worked Elkhorn No. 2
up Dry Branch Hollow
Then soon after the layoffs,
his hopes depleted
he started spending more time
at the Dew-Drop Inn.
On the stool he thinks about when
young men asked him for jobs
and remembers how on payday
he counted his cash in piles.
Now he drives the narrow road
past a salvage crew stripping
the Big John Tipple
and watches sun glare
off empty steel rails
already coating with rust.
All the men he bossed
long ago quit waiting for change
so he stands there alone
staring at pock-marked signs,
listening to bees on ironweed
growing between the ties.

Joseph Caldwell

(*Sabbatical on Winifrede Hollow*, Trillium Press, 1993)

Money for a Pepsi

I have been drowning, fighting for a breath.
I have watched a coal beltline eat my fingertip.
      No, Honey.
           I don't have money
             for you
            a Pepsi.

Walter Lane

(*Appalachian Heritage* {review}, 2000)

Digging Deeper

A car grumbles past my high window,
Gray with the lung-eating dust,
The bumper sticker grinning,
"Coal miners do it underground,"
And I think about the mantrip,
The raw, flickering bulbs,
The color-coded cables,
Wires carrying death or life,
The black and shining face
Promising treasure
Under a four-foot roof
Breaking six-foot bodies and itself
When no one is watching
How terror is buried
In four-lettered courage
And the shoulder-shrug
Claiming that it's never raining
Under the ground.

Barbara Smith

A Miner's Chill

An east Kentucky miner leaves dark bits and pieces of skin
On the cold bath house floor,
Scrubbed there
By the strength of calloused hands.

Letting go a layer of black,
He's making ready
For the truck ride
Away from the drift mouth—home.

He stops for gas and a long vertical look
At a still-pretty, single attendant.
Softer shades of black day remain,
A name badge linking him and his labor.

But the surest sign
He mines coal
Is the coldness of a hand reaching for receipt,
Touching hers.

She would need to stare down the mineshaft,
To feel what he feels—
A chill
Only a miner can know.

Ken Slone

(*At Home in the Mountains*, Jesse Stuart
Foundation, 2001)

Coal Miners Off Duty

They sit at candy-striped tables
in Wendy's Old Fashioned Harmburgers,
small blue eyes lined
with mascara badges
cold cream could wipe off.
Great huge men
they crawl
through little
black
holes
so they can take their wives and kids
to Wendy's Old Fashioned Hamburgers.
They sigh.
Stiff butts creaking
against the hard red chairs,
they rub their small, mascaraed eyes
and yearn for the uniform dark
of hoot-owl shift.

Bonni McKeown

(*Pieces: A West Virginia Woman Looks at Love,
People, and Politics*, 1978)

Traveling Song

Inside darkness of rainy night
moving through myself,
flowing with my blood,
traveling as the native going back,
     lost-looking for home,
I follow as the rain soaks away the hills,
sinking into the ground,
merging into the hidden arteries
     of earth.

Miners, low-roof bent in Appalachia,
     in Wales,
we have always lived in the mist,
known hill country fog and brief,
     sudden sunshine.

Margaret McDowell

(*Our Song, Too*, 1974)

II

Disasters & Mining

Monongah, WV

*On December 6, 1907, the Fairmont Coal Co.
exploded, killing all of the Miners on the day
shift. The official count of 360 overlooked
many immigrants.*

1.

On December 6, I drive to this place
along Route 19, near the banks of the Tygart
and turn my car toward the wrinkled flow
of the West Fork River, and stop. The fresh snow
has begun to crest around rocks and debris.
In the water, old antifreeze bottles knock
against each other, like aimless chimes.

I looked at the river, which is gray
in the center, reflecting the sky between hills.
Isn't that always the sky in West Virginia?

2.

A spark ignites Black Damp, the methane blows,
flames rush from speck to speck—like a breath
of a surging dragon, licking the coal dust
suspended in haulageways, spitting fire,
reaving stout timbers, seeking, by instinct
like bones among fossils, devouring the faces
before they can scream, as the men duck,
are sucked into blazing entries or crouch
in a shelter of ash, by crimson steel cars.

3.

There's a meadow, filled with threadbare gray
of five hundred women in the snow. They sob

68

to the heavens, gaunt as the heavens are
in West Virginia. I ask them to leave,
for we're in danger from another explosion,
but the women won't go. Eyes starving
for news, they peer from snow-soaked scarves,
babushkas, chadors, prayer shawls.

The mine blows again, and the earth trembles
like the hide of a frightened mule.

4.

I blink and the West Fork River
seems to sizzle beneath the snow's touch.
The fog drifts off down the river,
between two banks of melting snow,
toward Morgantown and Pittsburgh,
cities of what once was—

the smoke and fire
in the human heart.

5.

This spring, I'll drive out to this place,
this wilderness between rivers.
The meadow will fill with survivors, and
five-hundred threadbare women
will clutch their dusty lovers and go home.

David Salner

(*Elixir* {review}, 2006)

Monongah

*(December 6, 1907, Marion County, West Virginia,
on the Monongahela River)*

Tell in the wind of the singing of sorrow;
Read on this whiteleaf the dirge of the poor;
Stand on the bank of this north-flowing river;
Mark with your silence a cross on its shore.

Say that these men were from far-distant countries;
"Hunkies" and "Tallies," and Russian and Pole,
Welshman and Irish—then some from the mountains—
And all of them diggers, who dug in the coal.

See how they come to the portals that morning,
Lamps on their foreheads and lunch pails that shine;
See how they stand for a hesitant moment;
Watch how they vanish down into the mine.

Hear the first blast—how it shudders the mountains—
Now hear the others—the feedings of hell—
Then, like an answer, the cries of the women—
And all in a second—how utter it fell.

The four that got out. . . say they died in the morning,
Or else when the midnight had crawled on the shore;
And the gravediggers dug in the earth of the frost runes;
And each of the shanties—a wreath on the door.

Then say that they came where the torch seemed to beckon,
That torch by the ocean as bright as the sun—
Count on the stars over ill-starred Monongah;
Reckon the death toll:

Three-sixty-one.

Louise McNeill

(*Elderberry Flood*, Elderberry Books, 1979)

1907, West Fork Valley, West Virginia

The whine of the hoist cage
Sends a message
Through the camp.

Slowly it rises, bringing up a body.
It's not weighed down,
It's just somebody's body
Creaking up the shaft.

"Who's hurt, Mama?"

"Hush, child."

"Are they bringing up a body?
Is it somebody's body?"

"Hush."

"What's under the canvas, Mama?
Is somebody dead, Mama?
Is that a leg, Mama?
Whose leg is it, Mama?"

"Hush, child."

"Can we go home now, Mama?
Ain't we going home now, Mama."

"Hush."

Phyllis Wilson Moore

(*Whetstone,* Spring 1990)

Farmington No. 9

We lie here
waiting for the men
with rubber blankets
to take us up
and put us down again.

Remember us
when you fly over mountains
and land in a city at night
and see the thousand things
they've done
with our eyes.

Lloyd Davis

(*Wild Sweet Notes*, edited by Kirk Judd
and Barbara Smith, Publishers Place, 2000)

View from the Farmington Christmas Tree Farm

From the Old Cemetery, the highest point
where copperheads sun themselves on tombstones,
surrounded by a hundred thousand Norway spruce,
you see the portal of Mine Number 9.
In late November, 1968,
nights at a miner's home,
you study the underground map,
know where the men are,
the men who will never return to Farmington
or Mannington, Plum Run, Monongah or Idamay.
Explosive flames throw heavy shadows.

As you harvest under the black smoke tower,
Vexar-wrapped, fresh cut trees lie stacked in town
waiting for uneasy truck drivers.
Wives together also wait;
barely taste Red Cross soup; dislike reporters;
take comfort from their children, parents, sisters,
brothers, NFL great, Sam Huff.
A voice says, "Jimmy's here now. It will be all right."
But A. James Manchin speaks
without projection or alliteration.
Not even "Uncle Jimmy" could make this right.

Mary Lucille DeBerry

(Traditions: A Journal of West Virginia Folk
Culture and Educational Awareness, 2006)

Buffalo Creek

The river belches out its dead, and they flood
the banks with dragging feet asking *What happened to us?*
What happened? It was morning and time
for breakfast. They gather in puddles outside your window
and listen closely for the *hmm-click* of the burner
as you cook your morning eggs. They gather in the yard
behind the church and in the Foodland parking lot. They gather
in the fog and rockdust and orange pall of tipple lights.
They gather on the banks from Kistler to Chapmanville
to Salt Rock and the Ohio and ask *What happened?*
It was morning and time for breakfast.

Jason Frye

Buffalo Creek

> {T}he Buffalo Creek disaster in West Virginia in February,
> 1972. . . . produced a major human tragedy with the loss of
> hundreds of lives because of the careless administration of
> a gob pile dam, which wiped out a whole valley.
>   Richard B. Drake, *A History of Appalachia*

I

There may have been a girl,
fourteen or fifteen, waking up just then in a dark room
filled with pink chenille, gold stars from teachers,
a Sunday-school collage with a pipecleaner boat, dirty cottonball sky
and glitter sprinkled over blue construction paper under the feet
of a mimeographed Jesus walking on the water—
too much childhood in the room for it not to pinch, even in her sleep,
like church shoes squeezed on over everyday socks.
She may have waked with a start a little before 8:00
from a dream about a beautiful room, spare and open to the air,
in a house she brought by opening doors. Maybe she sat up—
long-haired and loose, her first beauty come on her—and suddenly
          knew
that she was someone, and something else might be true.

Then the mountains all around must have seemed to her a storm
of waves poised to crash, terrible undertow cast in stone,
but she was up to it, could sail under her own power,
lift and go. As daylight seeped in through the seams
of the room maybe she felt less sure, but she was marked
by the dream of air and space. She may have flopped back down
on her side, propped up on one elbow to see
what the weather was like outside the window beside her bed
in the small built-on second-story room. A raven, just one,
may have flown across her line of sight, skidded to a stop in the cold
wet of the back yard, flicked its head back over its shoulder then
          taken off again,

easy over the mountain. And maybe she thought of Noah,
or maybe she didn't, as she lifted her chin slightly to watch it go
and willed it to bring her a sign of the world.

II

Say her mother was downstairs in the kitchen
standing in the open door of the refrigerator, thinking about eggs
and work—inside of an hour, she was thinking, she'd be at Pittston,
    filing
disciplinary reports and safety reports she tried not to read
and workman's comp claims she tried never to read, the way she
    never
read the obituary page, though the names sometimes jumped out at
    her, faces
resurrected from her old yearbook, caught off guard by a sudden
    flash
and someone telling them to smile. Or she may have been thinking
    about eggs
in baskets made the old way, the way Aunt Mandy taught her,
how Aunt Mandy used to stand at the fence, an old egg basket on
    one elbow
ballasting the jutted-out ledge of a hip seating a child
crooked in the other. Could be then she thought of the work baskets
    filled
with yarn and thread and patches, the ways women find
of holding together what's coming apart, or maybe of babies left
in baskets on doorsteps. Maybe that made her think
of Moses and bulrushes so that as she called upstairs
for the girl to come down before the eggs got cold
she thought she heard a rush of water in the distance
and something small crying.

III

The father must have been at work on the longwall, graveyard
shift about to be over. Still February, but already

moles and groundhogs would be turning up
clumps of dirt, making the yard look like a kid's game, a maze
on the back of a cereal box—*Help the rabbit find his way home.*
He worked too goddamn hard to make house payments
to let the yard go to pot on account of critters. *Nothing else
to do, goddamn it*—and maybe here he slammed the machine
harder into the coalface, rehearsing the argument
he'd have with his wife and daughter—*Nothing
to be done but plug up one hole and run the garden hose
down the other.* It's how the bosses kept their heads
above water: show no pity for things that burrow.

IV

If the raven looked back in a minute, or two, he saw failed arks,
houses smacking into bridges and power lines, saw them fly
into the air, burning and drowning at once in the blank
roaring maw of that black wave
that hit the valley floor like God slamming the door,
jarring the whole world off the wall, and the stars,
with only a smattering of glitter riding
the wave, and no babies in baskets, and no one
walking on the water.

Diane Gilliam Fisher

(*Shenandoah* {review} Summer 2005)

Blood Money

This blood rolling down my arm
is from the wounds of a dollar bill
that cut my fingers as I touched it.
The blood runs down my elbows
and drips off onto the sand.
Mr. Pittston is kicking dirt over it,
swearing
there are no names written
on that dollar bill.

All this is the result
of thinking too much
about a Law Suit
proving me of
"The Survival Syndrome":
I get money
but none of the dead are resurrected.

Gail Amburgey

(*Soupbean: An Anthology of Contemporary
Appalachian Literature*, Mountain Union Books, 1977)

Spring in Glen Jean

so when his buddies brought
his lunchbucket home
she looked off sad
and kind of flighty
sitting there almost numb
burning the corners of her twisted hanky
with a Chesterfield cigarette
creating her own dogwood legend

Bob Snyder

(*Mucked*, edited by Bob Henry Baber
and Jim Webb, Hesperus Press, 1978)

Almost Heaven, Almost Hell

Which
Part of

West, by God
Virginia

Do you
live in?

(from found poems, compiled for the people
of the Tug Valley, by Bob Henry Baber and
Jim Webb)

(*Mucked*, edited by Bob Henry Baber and Jim
Webb, Hesperus Press, 1978)

As the Dust Settles

anger builds like
methane gas, that gas
that exploded sixteen hours ago
down there, in where,
thank God, you weren't working,

useless, fury, for
I have no walls to blow,
no shafts to block,
no mantrips or belts
to smash, destroy.

just this anger.

no meters,
no gauges
could predict it,
could have carried away
the gas instead of

dead bodies
that even now
as I imagine them,
turn anger to sorrow,

and I find myself
with you

crying

Barbara Smith

The Miner's Widow Testifies at the Black Lung Trial

Yes, I'll tell the truth.
I always tell the truth and
here it is.

38 years underground and
down in his back
the last fifteen.

You want to know how
he was in his breathing?

Well, he gasped and wheezed
and smothered all the time.
He'd be up restless all
night. Couldn't put out a
garden or mow the grass.
No yardwork, no housework
except I did it or the kids
did it or we hired it done.

Phlegm built up all night
and choked him of a morning.
Every morning he'd drink him
a big cup of black coffee,
and go out in the yard and
vomit it all up, the worse
looking stuff you ever saw,
green and gray with black
streaks in it and some
blood sometimes. But
then he'd breathe a little
better and get through
the day.

He stayed nervous. The
least little thing would
get him so tore up he'd have
to get off by himself.

I guess you'd be nervous too
if you had trouble getting
the breath of life itself
in and out of your lungs,
slowly smothering to death
every minute of every hour
of every day of what was
left of your life, and you
knew who'd done it to you,
and why they done it, and
you couldn't do much of
anything about it except
file for these benefits.

Did he smoke? Yes, he smoked.
But cigarettes aren't made
out of coal dust. He had coal
dust on his lungs and that's
what took him away. The mines
put the dust there not the
cigarettes.

He wasn't perfect, but
he was always good for working.
Took all the hours he could
get, never missed unless he
just had to. He was serious as a heart attack
about taking care of his family.

Many times I've seen him drag
himself off to the mines when
I knew he shouldn't have.
We tried to keep him home but
he'd just go on out.

The bosses came to his funeral
and said what a good employee
he was.

I know they made a lot of money
off his work.

They owned the mines.
It looks like they could have
done better at keeping the dust
down. And now they're fighting
the case with lawyers to beat
me out of the benefits.

Well, I know what killed him.
I don't care what their doctors and lawyers say.
It was their mines killed him,
choked and smothered to death
on coal dust and thick green phlegm.

John Taylor

Long Story

> To speak in a flat voice
> Is all that I can do.
> —James Wright, "Speak"

I need to tell you that I live in a small town
in West Virginia you would not know about.
It is one of the places I think of as home.
When I go for a walk, I take my basset hound
whose sad eyes and ungainliness always draw
a crowd of children. She tolerates anything
that seems to be affection, so she lets the kids
put scarves and ski caps on her head
until she starts to resemble the women who have to dress
from rummage sales in poverty's mismatched polyester.

The dog and I trail the creek bank with the kids,
past clapboard row houses with Christmas seals
pasted to the windows as a decoration.
Inside, television glows around the vinyl chairs
and curled linoleum, and we watch someone old
perambulating to the kitchen on a shiny walker.
Up the hill in town, two stores have been
boarded up beside the youth center and miners
with amputated limbs are loitering outside
the Heart and Hand. They wear Cat diesel caps
and spit into the street. The wind
carries on, whining through the alleys,
rustling down the sidewalks, agitating
leaves, and circling the courthouse steps
past the toothless Field sisters who lean
against the flagpole holding paper bags
of chestnuts they bring to town to sell.

History is one long story of what happened to us,
and its rhythms are local dialect and anecdote.
In West Virginia a good story takes awhile,
and if it has people in it, you have to swear
that it is true. I tell the kids the one about
my Uncle Craig who saw the mountain move
so quickly and so certainly it made the sun
stand in a different aspect to his little town
until it rearranged itself and settled down again.
This was his favorite story. When he got old,
he mixed it up with baseball games, his shift boss
pushing scabs through a picket line, the Masons
in white aprons at a funeral, but he remembered
everything that ever happened, and he knew how far
he lived from anywhere you would have heard of.

Anything that happens here has a lot of versions,
how to get from here to Logan twenty different ways.
The kids tell me convoluted country stories
full of snuff and bracken, about how long
they sat quiet in the deer blind with their fathers
waiting for the ten-point buck that got away.
They like to talk about the weather,
how the wind we're walking in means rain,
how the flood pushed cattle fifteen miles downriver.

These kids know mines like they know hound dogs
and how the sirens blow when something's wrong.
They know the blast, and the stories, how
the grown-ups drop whatever they are doing
to get out there. Story is shaped
by sound, and it structures what we know.
They told me this, and three of them
swore it was true, so I'll tell you
even though I know you do not know
this place, or how tight and dark the hills
pull in around the river and the railroad.

I'll say it as the children spoke it,
in the flat voice of my people:
down in Boone County, they sealed up
forty miners in a fire. The men who had come
to help tried and tried to get down to them,
but it was a big fire and there was danger,
so they had to turn around
and shovel them back in. All night long
they stood outside with useless picks and axes
in their hands, just staring at the drift mouth.
Here's the thing: what the sound must have been,
all those fire trucks and ambulances, and the sirens,
and the women crying and screaming out
the names of their buried ones, who must have
called back up to them from deep inside
the burning mountain, right up to the end.

Maggie Anderson

(*A Space Filled with Moving*, University
of Pittsburgh Press, 1992)

Numbers

The sky turns
an illuminated grey
this afternoon
behind each window of the house

suspended like an amulet

and I am waiting in my kitchen
drinking tea
waiting for the latest
news.

Among other things today
hope was officially forbidden
78 miners
nine hundred feet down.

It is easy to feel
the necessary sorrow

this formal tragedy of ciphers
coming as it does
at 5 o'clock
from a white cube of abstractions

the radio
placed casually
crossways on the refrigerator.

Later commentators
will assure me
it was a day like all days.
I will have had another

cup of pale tea
drifting between what is common
in the black jeweled earth
      of west virginia
and this grey sky

     And at other times
I may stop
trying to understand the words
for a number of men
a number of feet deep
     isolate at this
     afternoon echo
     of water falling in a sink

as the radio begins knowingly
      dealing in numbers.

     Harley Elliott

(*Working Classics*, edited by Peter Oresick
and Nicholas Coles, University of Illinois Press, 1990)

Azrael on the Mountain

the crane used in mountaintop removal coal mining

Azrael spoke
the angel of one wing, featherless
come from the sun where God, effortless
lavishes heat and light
and demands the soul
whom Azrael has come to fetch
but fell clumsily
a wing torn loose and lost
a feathery sea-swell, glistening black
gloriously iridescent on the horizon

and Azrael, winged like a maple seed
whirled and fell
his feathers wrenched away
lingering like fiery cirrus in the twilight
his gray down the darkness coming on

and Azrael fell, skeletal and gigantic
a shambling scandal to the glory of God
who is forever radiant, forever the light of now
and Azrael woke to the scaffolding of his single wing
girded against the sky
and cried out—
Majesty, where am I?
What is Thy will?

but God, who cannot abide a fault or a flaw
shuddered and turned away
gazing, instead, at the galaxy
intent on the milky hymn
the swirl and spiraling of eternity.

Azrael looked about, bewildered—
where was the soul he was to sunder from its self
where the standers-by at the bedside
where the silent grief, the choked sobs
the watery sorrow on the face

and how was he to pause
great, gray-winged and magnificent
his talons poised above the soul
to seize it and soar—
the lamentation of the living
the chaos of wind and wing-beats
rising toward God.

Azrael, bereft of duty
one-winged, plucked, absurd, ignored by God
drags himself in his grandeur
grotesque, insanely on the mountain top
back and forth.

Victor Depta

(*Azrael on the Mountain*, Blair Mountain Press, 2002)

Yesterday's News

It's barely a new year and tragedy
fills the news. Coal miners missing
in an explosion, families waiting
in a white church where days stumble
into nights, cameras panning to the
black mouth of the mine. Until a moment
when they hear that the men survived.

One girl shown over and over on tv
shouts "they're alive." It's not her fault.
People hug and cry until the truth
bleeds into words, this time,
miners are dead.
Are dead. Are dead.
One woman asks
if anyone can believe in God.

Someone official can't explain any
of it away but blames a failure
of words spoken and words heard
underground, through rock, heard
in their hearts. Someone else vows
to make sure it doesn't happen
again but everything does
happen again and then,
soon enough, again.

Sandra Marshburn

Shannon Wamsley Talks about the Sago Mine Disaster

When the lightning strikes I shatter Elton's coffee cup.
Venus visible this week, the moon new, I'd been
staring out across the black, rinsing breakfast dishes.
I race down to the mine, my mind
a-swirl like the Buckhannon River.
Lightning's queer in January here.

Elton stands there, face black, but safe and sound.
I'm bound to joke, say some trite thing
about our lives cheating the blast,
when Anna, last of the wives comes up crying
Elton's face goes slack before trying some
comfort, sharing some word of hope he's heard.

I realize her Randy's still trapped and my own heart
goes cold inside my quilted vest, Christmas plunder
Elton's coal wages bought. "The wages of sin" comes to mind
I try to shake the thought, but how?
I have my husband. The others wait.
How can you sort happiness from guilt?

Guilt and thanks—what if it had been a normal day?
His crew waited ten minutes for a buggy big enough to take them in.
Ten minutes, I hear Elton say, he'd have been round that turn.
Ten minutes, he'd been trapped inside.
Ten minutes, I'd be waiting with the other wives.
Ten minutes, if it had been a normal day.

Elton says when it starts getting hot, he never does see fire.
Just hears this roar and feels a rushing wind.
Heat and soot, dust and smoke keep coming
clammy air where you can't make out your hand or breathe.
Monitors beep and blink and men fear they're fixed to die
and all the time, this rushing wind. He says you feel your way along.

Sitting in his pickup holding vigil, I can't help but fit my
      pinky to the hollow
of his cheek. At two a.m.—I must have nodded off—I wake
      a-shiver
not from cold, but from how long the other wives must
      wait and wonder.
In the dim light a sliver of moon provides,
I stare as Elton snores, for a moment deep in sleep.
I used to fret his noise had woke me up.

              Beth Wellington

. . . Sago, Aracoma . . .

I was born and raised
far away and away   from coal country
—the nearest I came was Shenandoah, PA
where a friend from my neighborhood   in North Philly
took me
              when we were just kids
for a double date   with his cheerleader girlfriend
                    and *her* cheerleader girlfriend
  (didn't work out at all   for me *or* her friend)
  so I know
I don't know   much, not really
about what coal miners and their folks are up against
not in general
and not in a situation
like the recent
                  underground explosion   out at West Virginia's
non-union, Sago Mine   January 2nd
and the underground fire   later that month
over at the non-union
                        Aracoma coal mine, in Melville
but I for sure   understand
the contemptuous   the smug lies, and evasions
of those who profit
                    one way or another   from the work
endurance   and the losses of others
I understand
              the mine-owner spokesman   on the radio
who admonished us
              all of us   to give thanks to God
for saving one life
                    though snuffing out   twelve
this time—I know *him*—
and the other   mine-owner spokesman

telling us that the company was   saddened
by the loss of two *more* lives
and would focus
                    on comforting the families
I've been hearing these spokesmen   mostly men
all my life—
we all have   haven't we
that much, at least   unites us
doesn't it

Harry Gieg

In Sago

The preacher said, Jack Weaver scrawled *Jesus Saves*
in the coal dust, on the side of the mantrip
before they rode down into the mountain,
the part God made black.
He said some of them men never left West Virginia,
that Junior Hamner grew up raising beef
just above where he died.
He said those men worked as brothers
doing what needed done,
their sweat holy.
If coal fails the country fails.

That crew was tough,
two miles in when hell exploded,
lightning struck, the fire damp lit.
Belt man died right then.

Smoke and gas rolled down the shaft;
acrid dust settled on tongues.
They heaved timbers, hung brattice cloth on spads,
cocooned in a cross-cut.

An old miner in my Bible study
said they could have just walked out
the same way they came,
following the rails
down 2 Left and back Main
but they were taught *barricade in.*
They knew that oxygen in their rescuers
was good for one maybe two hours.

Lying side by side
in the cool damp black,
the startling silence, broken by
popping coal ribs.

Ten maybe hours passed.
Talk of Jesus and cards drifted.
Not knowing if some dead already,
Toler found an insurance application in his pocket,
wrote loose and jagged,
a blackened apparition saying
It isn't bad, it's just like sleep.
Tell all—I see Them on the other side.
I love you.

Who'd they see?
Aunt Maydell serving buttermilk and cornbread

wild John taking his with honey.
What were they thinking on? NASCAR and horsehoes,
a daughter in a red jacket
now photographed on the front of USA TODAY
crying by the tipple.

When Jesus died, the earth cracked and trembled right then,
not before, rocks split, the sky darkened
and they barricaded him inside the mountain
but he got free, came walking on the outside,
as we prayed you would,
thirteen cap lamps bobbing out,
piercing our darkness
with an unbelievable story.

Cheryl Denise

Deep Mine Memorial

Nellis, West Virginia

Flash—and dust in the jagged dark.
Two shafts of light stir through cough
and moan, a third fixed overhead.
Risen figure throws off his gear:
neck burns, battery leaking acid.
He takes the light of the fallen man
and looks in his face. A column of coal

upholds the world remaining.
Silence, then speechlessness. Hoping
for oxygen in rocky voids, they wear
their ragged burial clothes. Inside
this flood-lit installation, a mile
beneath a company town, visitors
talk low. Family names float

in plexiglass across the coal, grim
etch of alphabet. The two miners
conserve the air their friend
has left them. Schoolchildren read
the faces and poses against curtains
gathered back: the story recast
in shadows above ground.

A.E. Stringer

III

Families & Community

Suffering Job

Preacher speaks of sores and suffering Job as
bumblebees bump the great glass windows. Outside
the earth shakes and moves; the railroad runs long steel tracks
beside the church. Old men cough as the old
women lean forward in the pews. All the bees fly
away.

Preacher speaks of sores and suffering Job, but
his voice is lost with the coming of the train.
Coal bits hit the great glass windows and the sound
echoes up each aisle. Old men turn their heads, they
watch the cars roll by. The old women can only look
away.

Brooke Haynes

Coal Camp Supper

Lift the lid
on the pot of pintos,
cooked all day
with a chunk of salt bacon.
Dip the ladle in and stir,
make sure the beans
aren't sticking.
The beaded cornpone is cooling
on the window sill.
The woman's eyes are red and smarting,
blind with tears,
from slicing a yellow onion.

Homemade sour kraut and pickled hot peppers
grace the evening table,
also a crock of fresh-churned butter,
Granny brought from the dairy.

Fried potatoes in the cast-iron skillet
are crisp and brown.
Black coffee is perked and waiting,
Glasses of sweet milk and buttermilk sit on the kitchen counter,

Fried apples simmer on the back burner,
Blackberry cobbler bubbles in the oven.

Sarah L. Cornett-Hagen

Pearlie Tells What Happened at School

Miss Terry has figured since we are living
in a coal camp, we ought to know geology,
which is learning about rocks. Every day
we got to bring in a different rock
and say what it is. Even our spelling words
is rock words, like *sediment* and *petrified*.
Yesterday, Miss Terry says, *Who can use*
"petrified" in a sentence? and Walter Coyle
raises his hand, which, he don't never
say nothing. He's a little touched, Walter is,
ever since his uncle Joe—he was the laughingest,
sparkliest-eyed man you ever seen—ever since Joe
got sealed in at Layland and they ain't never
gonna know if he got burnt up or gassed
or just plain buried. So Walter says,
and he don't never look up from his desk,
he says, *Miss Terry, can a person get petrified?*

Miss Terry thinks he is sassing her, 'cause she
don't know about Joe Coyle, and about
how Walter don't never sleep no more
nor hardly eat enough to keep
a bird alive, as his mama says.
Miss Terry sends him to the cloak room
but Walter, he just walks on out. I reckoned
that was the last we'd see of Walter.
He come back this morning, though, pockets
filled with rocks, and with a poke full of rocks.
Spreads them all out on Miss Terry's desk
'fore she even asks. *Well, alright,* she says,
suppose you tell us what these are.

Walter stirs the rocks around a bit, so gentle,
picks up a flat, roundish one and lays it
agin his cheek. *This here*, he says,
is the hand.

Diane Gilliam Fisher

(*Kettle Bottom*, Perugia Press, 2004)

Grandfather

it says much for your life,
old man of leather, tobacco, earth and flannel
        that sixteen years after your death
        I still long for the comfort
    of your calloused, scarred-knuckle hands
from a hundred saws in migrant logging camps
        from a hundred picks in dog hole mines;
I remember stories of sawdust and blood, coal and bone
        I want to slip you your whiskey bottle
                stashed in the pantry,
        pick you the reddest banana peppers,
        hear you tell the moons to plant by
old man of leather, tobacco, earth and flannel;
    tell me again of your father who lost family and land
        as lone Union soldier of five Southern sons,
        tell me of your mother's fugitive father
            who climbed the mountains to escape
                the deadly march to Oklahoma,
tell me again of your marches and blacklistings,
        how you never signed a yeller dog contract
old man of leather, tobacco, earth and flannel
        once I held up oak saplings in the sun
    you skinned down to bridge a mountain stream;
            we are still working together
you bared your history and held it up to the light
        now I am laying a bridge back to you.

                        Mary Joan Coleman

            (*Take One Blood Red Rose*, West End, 1978)

Harlan Portraits

I've seen beauty in Harlan,
In the trailing arbutus,
The dogfennel and pennyroyal
In the fence corners,
And in forests dressed
In a foliage of
Rattleweed and ditney.
I've seen beauty when
Grey winter strokes his beard
With bony-white fingers,
And trees are skeletons
Of summer's glory...

But beauty
Never visits the coal diggers.
They live in the coal camps—
Dirty shanties,
Stinking privies,
Grunting pigs,
And slop buckets...

Gaunt-eyed women
With dull hopeless faces
Cook soggy wheat biscuits.

Tall gaunt men
Eat soggy bread
And fat meat,
Gulp down black coffee,
Work all day—

Digging, digging,
Everlastingly digging.
Grime and dirt
And digging.
In their dreams they dig
And smell unpleasant
Odors.

For beauty
Is a stranger
To the coal camps . . .

Don West

(*Deep, Deep Down In Living*, 1932)

Carrying the Kerosene
Coal Miner's Daughter, 1933

This is Pursglove, West Virginia
where the tipple's pyramid
announces something sacred's
taken from this valley.

Past ten steps and blind slats
lining the company store,
a miner's little daughter walks,
face down, dust soft as ribbons in her hair.

It's her turn to carry kerosene
for the lamps. She wears a white sundress,
dull brown shoes laced to her ankles,
the forwardness of meadow wildflowers.

With each step her weight bends
the grass, splits the tipple's shadow.
Ebony chunks swell like bread loaves
in rail cars bound for cities she will never see.

Morning glories are blue curtains
pinned to an abandoned porch.
They quiver and hang faded at the pane.
The child's life is a rustle in a dogwood's petticoat.

She'll outlive the tipple's empty belly,
the slack jaw of the ridge.
Beyond this moment, sense her breath,
warm as oven biscuits, her pink body

curled in a poster bed, her name:
Dreama, Dreama. When you are five
and your Mama calls, you hurry from quilts,
button your dress, risk details of early darkness,

green eyes of small animals, snorting deer.
You fetch kerosene in a can, witness the miracle:
your father's blackened face
glowing, flawless, in the light.

Jeanne Bryner

(*Blind Horses*, Bottom Dog Press, 1999)

Mining Camp Residents,
West Virginia, 1935

They had to seize something in the face of the camera.
The woman's hand touches her throat as if feeling
for a necklace that isn't there. The man buries one hand
in his overall pocket, loops the other through a strap,
and the child twirls a strand of her hair as she hunkers
in the dirt at their feet. Maybe Evans asked them to stand
in that little group in the doorway, a perfect triangle
of people in the morning sun. Perhaps he asked them
to hold their arms that way, or bend their heads. It was
his composition after all. And they did what he said.

Maggie Anderson

(*Cold Comfort*, University of Pittsburgh
Press, 1986)

Coal Blue Tattoo

I dreamed of my grandfather, pale skinned and hatless,
Dressed in blue and gray.
He walked along Van Lear sidewalks,
Stooped, stood straight and tall
In the days of his youth—as yet unburdened.

Why he did not see the miners
Who passed him by
I went without understanding.
In my dream I saw them as clearly
As I saw the color of their eyes and his.

Time was on the move in my dream.
Papaw was to and from the drift mouth, unseeing,
As mine ponies gone blind out of the mine,
Their heads forever bent—scraped and bleeding—their hide
        dust darkened,
Then washed in gray-bright light outside the mine.

Papaw's life passed in my dream
Without his taking note of his fellow miners' bent backs
From breast auguring low coal.
He noticed only the sides of miners' faces
That bore no scars.

But I could see their bowed backs
And the way their eyes never quite adjusted to the light.
I could see their faces—
Both sides of their faces.
All were temporarily discolored from the coal dust.

Some, though, wore a permanent scar
From being too near the powder blast,
Close enough to the blast
That had come on unexpectedly strong,
That their faces had been forever tattooed coal blue.

We see what we choose to see.
Papaw never saw the scar he came to bear in my dream.
I wish he had had more choices.
I wish I had dreamt of him—his strength restored.
I wish I could dream again in black and white.

Ken Slone

(*Cut Thru Review*, 2002)

Best House They Was Ever In

(Retired Coal Operator)

In these mountains, there was coal,
And the World War looming—
Railroads just begun to roll—
Prices—they were booming.

Now with *coal*, it doesn't come
Running from a spigot.
Miners—they need a home
While they work to dig it.

And this country—back awhile—
Barren as November:
Not a town for thirty mile.
Nothing here but timber.

Miners couldn't help *themselves*—
Even build a hovel.
All they furnished on the job—
Just their pick and shovel.

Built them each a Jenny Lind,
Had them painted yellow—
Best house they was ever in—
Cabins—up the hollow . . .

Then a store so they could eat.
Then their kids, a teacher.
Built their church and graded school.
Even hired the preacher.

Now, I know the things they tell,
Grudges some still harbor—
Had to do it. Did it. Well?
Even got the barber.

With the shoestring that we had—
God, we had to hump it . . .
Call it *good* or call it *bad*—
Like it or you lump it.

Louise McNeill

(*Elderberry Flood*, Elderberry Books, 1979)

Coal Pickers

They walk the steep mine road at first light,
stopping for breath by laurel or spill bank.
They touch slate or stir dark pools
of water with walking sticks.
All day their fingers curl around coal.

I sit now in my own ashen dusk
and hear feet scraping shale or old timber.
What they whisper near the old tunnel
is what I have remembered for years.
I turn with them as they turn toward home,
buckets filled, the sky around them like cold grates.

Harry Humes

(*The Way Winter Works*, University of
Arkansas Press, 1990)

In Kentucky

In Kentucky
where my ancestors have all lived,
except the ones from overseas
before the big crossing
of the Atlantic and their bloodline, before
their coupling with Cherokee,
we live and die by our hand, by the land—
become kin to the earth as much as if
its water is our blood,
its soil our cells,
and roots, my lands—
they go down deep
" 'pert near plumb thru to China."

My granddaddy's breath, death
depended on what he put into the ground
as well as what he took from it.
He worked the earth and mines with
equal sweat seeking, eking out another day's wage
profiting little.

He tried to live by burley alone
bedding, pegging, chopping, suckering, topping,
cutting, hanging, stripping—
back in the days when you tied your hands
in more ways than one.
The buyer's price never met the cost of living.

He stooped to mining never seeing sunshine,
yet he tried by digging, picking, shoveling
his way out of the hole.
It's a fact that scrip doesn't go
as far as scripture

because coal mines and company stores
don't allow for laying up treasures.

Granddaddy picked up a hoe at ten,
a cigarette at fifteen, and a miner's lamp
twenty years later.
In Kentucky
through decades we continue the legacy,
as we, like he, grow and smoke tobacco,
choke on coal dust until
payday
when we face the blackened breath of death
and die
the only way we've ever known how to live.

Sandi Keaton-Wilson

(*The Journal of Kentucky Studies*, 2005)

Coal Country

(an excerpt from the sequence)

What I can't remember, and what I can:
my mother washing coal dust from the necks
of Mason jars filled with last summer's jams
and vegetables, their lids and rings black
with grit, contents obscured then visible
beneath the touch of a damp flannel rag
she wiped across hand-printed labels,
then dipped again into an enamel pan
where gray water settled from suds to silt.
Those cloths were always discarded, never
used for dishes again, deemed unfit
for the kitchen. Fifty years are over
now: I've known sullied cloth and family:
how some stains never wash out completely.

Christina Lovin

(*Passenger* {review} 2006)

Tableau at a Company House on Slate Dump Row

A mother, forgetting the
window she faces
is not a dark mirror from
the other side,
looks up from the dishpan
into her own unguarded eyes.
Forgetting her young son
has gone out back
to fill the coal buckets, she lets her
hands go motionless
on chipped mugs and bowls
while she stares without restraint,
taking stark comfort
from recognition she finds
in her own reflection.

For one unwary moment
she gives in to constant backache
concealed at all times
from the children
as carefully as death and childbirth.
Wiping the hair off her forehead
with the back of a
roughened wrist
while she searches her face
for some unspecified promise,
she contemplates
the bleak hours ahead
and indulges herself in this brief
draft of rare self-pity.

The babies must be
sponged and put to bed.
The waiting mound
of clean wash, each piece

120

sprinkled down and tightly rolled,
must be ironed by the light
of the one dangling bulb.
The frayed collar
of her man's only decent shirt
must be ripped out, turned,
and stitched back in place.
She'll be working,
like as not, when he comes off
the late shift,
blackened with coal dust
and dead on his feet.

The boy, balancing along
warped planks with a
full bucket pulling
at each arm, glances up from
frost-slick footing
to look, without her knowledge,
upon his mother's naked gaze.
His stricken breath hangs
unstirred on the air.
Suspended in one cocoon
of chambered stillness,
her hands limp and warm
in greasy water,
his clenched and cold
on metal bails, they enact
the defining moment
of his childhood. From that
instant's pause in respiration,
though circumstances
change to prove it wrong,
he cannot shake the conviction
his mother's life is
one of despair.

Marietta Ball

Tanya

One day after school
I was running the tracks
back into the country
in early spring, sunlight
glazing the chips of coal,
old bottles and beer cans
shoaling the sides. I ran
for miles, stripped
to the belly, dogwood
odors in the air like song.

When I stopped for breath
I saw there were women
bending in the ferns.
They spoke in Polish,
their scarlet dresses
scraping the ground
as they combed for mushrooms,
plucking from the grass
blond spongy heads
and filling their pouches.

But the youngest one
danced to herself in silence.
She was blond as sunlight
blowing in the pines.
I whispered to her . . . Tanya.
She came when the others
moved away, and she gave me
mushrooms, touching my cheek.
I kissed her forehead:
it was damp and burning.

I found myself sprinting
the whole way home
with her bag of mushrooms.
The blue sky rang
like an anvil stung
with birds, as I ran
for a thousand miles to Poland
and further east, to see her
dancing, her red skirt
wheeled in the Slavic sun.

Jay Parini

(*Anthracite Country*, Random House, 1982)

Our Parents' Lives

(for my sister)

Now that they are long gone,
I dreamt they met in a tavern and sat
in a booth, under low light, unable to see
the miniatures of us in each other's eyes.

It was 1943 or so. His left wrist smashed
and poorly set, he could not fight
Nazis. She worried about the work
in West Virginia: coalmines, glass

or nickel plants were about all, if at all.
This dream woke me, yet lingered
like walking into a spider web
in the dark. My bed sheets felt like

theirs, in leftover sleep, one of those
odd things to think about.
I could sense his desire to be gentle
and hers to understand what he meant to her.

They were together again in me,
where he could find her high cheekbones.
She could feel his mustache. The mouth
and tail of the ouroboros

about to touch, I got out of there
and jumped on the bus. They waved-by
in the yellow convertible
I always wanted them to have.

Ron Houchin

Don't Come Down

In the alley between Route 910 and the dump
of burning cinder, I listened to the guys
sing a cappella all summer-night long
James Lee's sweet velvet voice drifted slow
and Billy hit low baritone notes that sunk
into darkness, deep like coal mines below
where our fathers droned made-up worksongs
that echoed *Don't come down here*

under the streetlight's dim yellow haze
after thirty years only shadows remain and I
call out the name of each faceless voice
that moved stars around a moon full of blue
gentry dreams soft as Donnie's falsetto
and when Harold's bass broke the earth moaned
Muscles groaned *Don't come down here*

when all the spirit voices that I have ever heard
are shadows singing down on the swing-shift
Frankie's faint tenor is a steady undertone
pulling with tired arms black bodies home
Like chunks of burnt desire that roll down the dark
Split open the burning coal pyre to expose
Cinder hearts turned to white ash
The song slows, dust blows
Don't go

Sheila L. Carter-Jones

(Pennsylvania Review, 1994)

Diamond Jenny #5

Pound River, 1959

Slick, shiny, and black
like seals,
they floundered, bobbed in eddies
among black, torrent-tumbled boulders.
Child eyes, wide in the cushioned
world of the Ford
wondered at boys sliding,
clean and blond,
into the river,
bobbing up shiny black,
slicked like seals
by coal dust.
"Oh! Why does their mama
let them play there?"
"Don't stare!"
scolded mother,
born of that place,
"It's the only river they have."
The light changed,
descent from the mountain continued.
But child eyes
visioned forever
boys—slick, shiny, and black
like seals—
floundering, bobbing among
black, torrent-tumbled boulders.

Jane Hicks

(*Blood and Bone Remember*, Jesse Stuart
Foundation, 2005)

Rememberin' Yesterday

Mama and me would pack
his lunchpail right after
we got done eatin' supper
'cuz sometimes Daddy would leave
before mama went to bed,
when it was still dark;
when I was still sleepin'.

Summers when it was hot;
when the doors and windows
all stood open to catch a breeze
Mama and me would dust every day;
watch the sky for smoke and run
down the road with the neighbors
if the hill shook, shivered, groaned,
or . . . if the church bells started ringin'.

Mama watched the clock;
sat on the front porch or walked
to the edge of the yard if Daddy was late.
There was times she sat and cried,
but I didn't know the reason.
When Daddy did pull in, she'd yell
"'bout time you got home old man."
He'd smile . . . I'd laugh.

Daddy kept an old tin can under the bed;
told me it was for my schoolin',
so I'd do better for myself;

maybe even have a big house
right in the middle of town,
or get a job at the state capitol
changin' laws.
I just wanted to live next door.
Daddy would say, "Nope,
not a chance girl, not for you."

I didn't understand then . . .
  I do now.

Debra Harmes Kurth

(*A Place of...Amazing Grace*, Art with
Words, 2006)

High School

When we were kids everything was plike—you know, play-like—
plike you're an Indian and I'm a cowboy and this here dirt
hump's my fort and this pole's my rifle and you take that
capwire and make a bow and these stickweeds'll be your
arrows. High school was like that, including mud pies, tea
sets ands scraggly-haired dolls whose eyes were connected
to iron weights in their heads.

You'd think after school we went home to places like Glenwood
Meadows and Oakview Hills instead of a coal camp that
was another pretend—pretend it was a home when you
knew damn well the Company owned it, you, the cold-water
spigot in the kitchen and the outhouse which was not much
bigger than a coffin on end with a hole underneath it.

High school—Christ—we pretended to type and bookkeep and vo-
tech out back where we made door plaques for our families
out of yellow pine, which is no easy task if your daddy's
name happened to be Zakrzewska.

We studied civics and algebra and biology—we had cheerleaders
and a football team—just like everybody in America—and
never once did I hear the word *coal*—not once—there was a
never-never land we got off the school bus to every morning,
a pretend place without camp houses, burning gob piles,
railroad sidings, tipples, rattling noise, coal dust, black creeks,
slate dumps, drift-mouths and mines on the ridges.

Damn! Who was that education for? Not us miners' kids and that's
why we were such dumbasses for the teachers—*why won't
they learn? Stupid hillbillies*—and we stared quiet and hostile-
eyed at the teachers and their pretend future, knowing that
where we come from labor don't pay in America.

Victor Depta

(*Azrael on the Mountain*, Blair Mountain Press, 2002)

Mr. Ollie Fighting the Wind

1.
Mr. Ollie was so skinny that his Adam's apple
poked out like a second chin
guiding and pulling him as he pushed down the alley
fighting the wind on ice cold country days
blizzard gusts threaten with spiny icicle fingers
that rip round his bony spool unraveling
tattered threads of a dusty blue Company Store coat
under his chin a snap is broken by the first wind
and flying fast furry ears flap back
on a black vinyl cap being nearly snatched from his head
and by the time Mr. Ollie would get to our house
his ears burned red with cold
like I watched him grow old and hunched over
coming up out of the coal mines.

2.
A bleak winter sun gives form to Mr. Ollie's shadow
moving slow, a tired pick and shovel criss-cross
his shoulder numbed from working his religion
in the dark and dust below
he believes in the earth
in the bituminous chunks of gold
that riddle his lungs like loose change
until he's bent over coughing in hacks
and shoveling up thick dark phlegm
on chilly sleepless nights
restless, rolling over, nearly choking
and groping for his rusted companion
Mr. Ollie spits a powerful prayer
into the bedside Maxwell House coffee can

and wiping his mouth with the back of his hand
he curses the coal black demon heaving in his chest
and only a little does he rest before rising again
to fight the wind to our house.

Sheila L. Carter-Jones

(*Pittsburgh and Tri-State Anthology*, 1992)

Christmas in Coaltown

Tonight the men lift pokes instead of coal.
Their backs are puzzled by the lack of weight
And wish it were as easy lifting slate.
This work is play and good for a miner's soul.

They ride in the company truck by every door
Opening as they approach from the house below.
The fire spreads across the bluish snow
Tinting bearers of gifts from the company store.

And not a man but wishes these light sacks
Of nuts and candy and sweet tangerines
Were costlier gifts to suit the children's dreams,
Toys, and clothes to wear upon their backs.

But the men laugh. They laugh and they spread cheer
To the kid who takes a bag and darts back in
Behind the window, sending out his grin
They may not laugh again the rest of the year.

Billy Edd Wheeler

(*Song of a Woods Colt*, Droke House, 1969)

Buffalo Creek

Trucks rumble up and down the hollow
spilling dust which coats crippled sassafras leaves
then sifts through screens like flour.
When it rains the dust
changes to a fine gray dough,
sticking to shoes
leaving tracks across the porch.
The Company says it has a permit—
operates within the law.
Trucks just keep coming on
coal in their open wombs
going past the hill.
The afternoon sun shines straight
on a grime plated yellow bicycle
leaning against the post
of the front porch
where an empty glider sits
under scaling white ceiling paint.
At dusk, a firefly
smothers in the dust covered grass.

Joseph Caldwell

(*Sabbatical on Winifrede Hollow*, Trillium
Press, 1993)

The Child's Song

The song hangs in coal smoke over rows of house on
    pink streets,
    fairytale pink made of burned mine waste
    that smells like sulphur, burning.
A small boy playing
in the ashes from coal stoves,
pushing his toy dump truck along
a gray-black path to the pink road,
    singing:
        "He has a truck, and
        he's gotta work,
        he's gotta work…"
The mother says,
    "He can't talk plain,
    but he sings clear."

                Margaret McDowell

    (*Our Song, Too*, 1974)

The Post Card

For my Grandfather

I got your card today—30 years too late,
found among old letters and moths' wings
undelivered and yellow with time.
I read the careful hand from a cheap ballpoint
carried in the pocket of your best shirt:

"Dear G., wish you were here with me
on this big ship living the life of Riley.
Been to Bob-Lo, rode the Wild Mouse,
your uncle Bob wouldn't let us pay for nothing.
He's making big money at McLouth Steel,
never dirties his hands.
Detroit's a big town; Pikeville wouldn't hold
all the winos on Jefferson Avenue.
It's worth the trip just to watch how the sun
comes out of the ground.
But I'm ready to come home—
guess it's true what they say about lonesome water.

P.S. Boy, don't spend your life under the hill;
they're hiring every day at Whitehead and Kale."

"Dear Grandpa, glad you had a good time
your first trip to the big city—
far from Big Shoal and Left Beaver
where you drove your breast auger into the
bowels of the mountain
until numbness eased the aching,
down on your knees as one in prayer,
the pale nimbus of your carbide lamp
unwrapping the folds of eternal night.

You spat Red Man, drank sassafras and coughed
No. 3 Elkhorn until your spine curved.
Your hands, bent and tough as shoe leather,
tattooed with the ink of centuries,
never failed to put beans on the table.

You saw the canary die in the black damp
and rode the death car when they finally
pulled the rock off Henry Hall
hearing for all time the stoic clacking of the wheels,
dreading what waited beyond that far pinpoint of light.

Hope you had a long, long day at Bob-Lo Island.
Hope you stayed until that Michigan sun
dropped and burned into Lake Erie.

I was there, Grandpa—in the big city,
loading magnesium on a Great Lakes Freighter,
cursing the fog-bound tugs lowing in the harbor.
I slept in a cold-water flat,
delivered hell fire on an ingot buggy,
drank Peach and Honey with the painted girls
on Henry Street.
I rode the Wild Mouse.

Sorry, Grandpa, but I'm under the hill:
High coal, good top, pouring black diamond on
The hoot-owl shift.
Boy that runs the miner said he'd like to meet the man
who could put in a shift with a damn breast auger.
Wish you were here.

P.S. It was you, Old Man, who warned me
about the taste of lonesome water.

G.C. Compton

Diamond Jenny #7

for Silas House

The county agent
feels more than hears
blasting from Jenny #8,
thinks of his children wading
cool, green creeks beneath
slippery shale cliffs, prays blast
schedules be safely memorized.

Days when rain drums
the canvas Jeep cover,
he hears rain pounding large
leaves and white herons
shrieking like tracer
fire across humid heavens.

Lesser of evils, skulking
jungles instead of bending
to mines or raising a crop
of Yankee young'ns in Detroit,
the GI Bill brought him up
sampling soil and replanting
stripped slopes where his
children play in cool, green creeks
upstream from black water.

Jane Hicks

(*Blood and Bone Remember*, Jesse Stuart
Foundation, 2005)

Honey

My father died at the age of eighty. One of the last things he did in his life was to call his fifty-eight-year-old son-in-law "honey." One afternoon in the early 1930's, when I bloodied my head by pitching over a wall at the bottom of a hill and believed that the mere sight of my own blood was the tragic meaning of life, I heard my father offer to murder his future son-in-law. His son-in-law is my brother-in-law, whose name is Paul. These two grown men rose above me and knew that a human life is murder. They weren't fighting about Paul's love for my sister. They were fighting with each other because one strong man, a factory worker, was laid off from his work, and the other strong man, the driver of a coal truck, was laid off from his work. They were both determined to live their lives, and so they glared at each other and said they were going to live, come hell or high water. High water is not trite in southern Ohio. Nothing is trite along a river. My father died a good death. To die a good death means to live one's life. I don't say a good life.

I say a life.

James Wright

(*This Journey*, Random House, 1982)

Spitting in the Leaves

In Spanishburg there are boys in tight jeans,
mud on their cowboy boots and they wear huge hats
with feathers, skunk feathers they tell me.
They do not want to be in school, but are.
Some teacher cared enough to hold them. Unlike
their thin disheveled cousins, the boys on Matoaka's
Main Street in October who loll against parking meters
and spit into the leaves. Because of them, someone
will think we need a war, will think the best solution
would be for them to take their hats and feathers,
their good country manners and drag them off somewhere,
to Vietnam, to El Salvador. And they'll go.
They'll go from West Virginia, from hills and back roads
that twist like politics through trees, and they'll fight,
not because they know what for but because what they know
is how to fight. What they know is feathers,
their strong skinny arms, their spitting
in the leaves.

Maggie Anderson

(*Cold Comfort*, University of Pittsburgh
Press, 2000)

Diamond Jenny #4
Mistress Mine

He spends his day-nights
moving within her darkness.
She, rounded and beautiful,
older than memory,
larger than our lives,
dangerously moist and deep,
like all women keeps her secrets,
her treasures
tucked way, deep inside,
Her hold on our lives
is complete.
My days and nights are filled
with waiting
and the fear
she may someday choose
not to return him
to me.

Jane Hicks

(*Blood and Bone Remember*, Jesse Stuart
Foundation, 2005)

Deep Mining

Think of this: that under the earth
there are black rooms your very body

can move through. Just as you always
dreamed, you enter the open mouth

and slide between the glistening walls,
the arteries of coal in the larger body.

I knock it loose with the heavy hammer.
I load it up and send it out

While you walk up there on the crust,
in the daylight, and listen to the coal-cars

bearing down with their burden.
You're going to burn this fuel

and when you come in from your chores,
rub your hands in the soft red glow

and stand in your steaming clothes
with your back to it, while it soaks

into frozen buttocks and thighs.
You're going to do that for me

while I slog in the icy water
behind the straining cars.

Until the swing-shift comes around.
Now I am the one in front of the fire.

Someone has stoked the cooking stove
and set brown loaves on the warming pan.

Someone has laid out my softer clothes,
and turned back the quilt.

Listen: there is a vein that runs
through the earth from top to bottom

and both of us are in it.
One of us is always burning.

                    Irene McKinney

(*Six O'Clock Mine Report*, University of
Pittsburgh Press, 1989)

Love in the Coal Mine

Once pulled past the black mouth
the girls melted into the sides of their lovers
who knew the slope, the trapdoors, the danger of euphoria.
Unbuttoning the descent with a flashlight
wasn't like choosing a hollow on the beach
where open sandstone cliffs could be your temporary fort
and white light poured through gaps in the blankets.

Love in the coal mine, though damp and hot,
wasn't like wrapping your legs around your love in Lost Lake—
him standing your sliding ground,
you leaning back to float your hair on the water
like a slip of woodsmoke. And underground
you could never find anything like a pair of quick tongues
cricketing by a campfire.

Down there it was a deathless weight
rolled over your eyes, a thickness
that filled your throat, making your breath grow ragged
like an untimbered ceiling. In the airless rooms
you could believe in a flickering, floating way out—
like stiffening vertebrae arching and rising
in the underbellied dark.

Suzanne Matson

(*Sea Level*, Alice James Books, 1990)

Sulphur Mud

daddy said
keep your feet out the creek
I said
I did
but they was stained orange and
like a crawdad in sulphur mud
I ran backwards
fast as I could
from Diane's switch
straight to the ditch
mamaw saw, said *watch which*
flowers you pick, packed with chiggers
Diane said
it figures
we gave 'em too much melon
now there ain't no tellin
'bout sticky faces in grimy places
and we giggled sittin top of the bench.

daddy said
don't lay in the road
I said
I ain't
but my face had stained
black like tar
Tasha stuck on her nose
makin me laugh
as orange water passed
and we hid up the hill
in the tree.

Brooke Haynes

Coming Out of Wal-Mart

The child, puny, paling toward albino,
hands fused on the handlebars of a new bike.
The man, a cut-out of the boy, gnome-like,
grizzled, knotted like a strange root,
guides him out, hand on the boy's shoulder.
They speak, but in language softer than hearing.

The boy steers the bike as if he steered
a soap bubble, a blown glass swan, a cloud.

On the walk they go still. Muzak covers them.
Sun crushes. The man is a tiny horse,
gentle at a fence. The boy's eyes are huge
as a fawn's.

He grips hard the orange and pink,
and purple and green striped handlebars,
smiling the fixed sweet smile of the sainted.

Mark DeFoe

(*Hollins Critic*, June 1993)

Miner's Wife

It starts even before first light tumbles
down West Virginia mountains when
hours are hushed and I'm preparing kids for
bus stops, kissing them off into darkness
metamorphosing into morning. It has always
been with me even twenty-four hours into this
new year preparing ham and cheese sandwiches
for his lunch pail this Monday; thermos full
of hot coffee; black no sugar.

Standing on the threshold of another week
measured in thirteen hour shifts, it intensifies
as I straighten the lapel of his jacket, speak of
preferences for supper and relish the security
of his arms around my waist before surrendering
him to the mistress of dark dank places
in the center of the earth.

Mid-morning is worst, the predictability of
soaps, gossip shared with wives of other miners
and those ghosts, whenever I am ironing, of
lifeless canaries that haunt these anxious hours
until footfalls at dusk drive them away.

James E. Cherry

Going Home to John's Creek

Dust covers our car,
beige turned gray and Effie
comes out on the porch
with a gun in her hand,

Not a criminal,
just protecting her land.
Company took her sister's
place, over on Singer's Mountain,

held the mineral rights

on some deed,
a hundred years old.
So, Effie don't know it's us,
her own kin a comin home

at two in the morning.

Reedy-Mo hops out
"Mamma, hit's jes me."
Effie lays that gun down
Starts to laugh and cry.

"Youins come on in here right now."

We drink coffee til five
and sing "I'll Fly Away"
Then lay down in the parlor
where the guest bed is.

We sleep beside
a Kimper mine.
First time in ten years
and Effie, she smiles,

"G'night, y'all. G'night now."

Wanda Campbell

Coal Buckets

Loaded coal buckets rumble toward the sun ball east on Eighty,
Headed for Route Twenty-Three and points north—
Counties of Johnson, Lawrence, and Boyd.

Losing their loads from under well worn tarps,
They are paving the shoulder with bits of black coal,
Marking the Big Sandy Valley as their own.

Coal trucks are rugged reminders of life
In these east Kentucky mountains.
Loud lessons learned only by those who grew up here.

Overloaded with the past,
They are difficult to brake
As they haul the mountains' wealth to the world.

Outsiders, taking a scenic route north, fear them,
Imagining their drivers to be different than they,
An unseen, dark-faced race.

Eighty tons lighter but never really empty,
Coal buckets speed south through the Big Sandy Valley,
To turn west on Eighty into the setting sun ball, home.

Ken Slone

(*At Home in the Mountains*, Jesse Stuart
Foundation, 2001)

God in Appalachia

Sits not on a throne
But a stack of mine timbers,
His lamp the only real light in dark lives
A mile or more under not-too-solid ground.

On a stack of mine timbers
He offers apple pie in the sky
After a lifetime or more under not-too-solid ground
With lunch buckets of cornbread and water.

His offer of apple pie in the sky
Appeals to the soul-hungry women
Who fill lunch buckets with cornbread and water
Before and during and after the altar call.

Appealing especially to soul-hungry women
He sits not on a throne but on mine timbers
Before and during and after the altar call
His lamp is the only real light in their dark lives.

Barbara Smith

(*Grab-a-Nickel*, Winter 2004/2005)

Mine

The year my dad's back
gave out, Doc Hadden read the tests
and sighed, "black lung" while mother
stood apron clad with hanky-pressed mouth,

dry eyed. Some months later came
her call, a blinking light left, found
upon my tired return from
a medical research cram.

I pulled the indexed notes, stacked
so neatly in my bag and sat,
listened to her words and flipped
through detail-crowded cards,

each a meticulous list
of disease and lethal symptoms.
I'd read their names, drop my eyes
test myself: Scrofula: tubercular

infection; impacts throat lymph glands.
At twenty, he'd followed his father
into the seams, ceilings dripping water. He'd lie
in mud, supine, nineteen working inches

lit only by his miner's lamp.
Yaws: chronic, relapsing infectious
illness; spirochete caused; cannot penetrate
skin. Influenza: virus; changes by mutation.

The day he told me the story of Macbeth,
the mine that blew a dark March day
and took his father's life, I knew the chain
would break. Pneumoconiosis: also known

as black lung disease; two forms—
simple and progressive massive fibrosis.
Miners who'd once gone below
in dark of early morning trudged

over those same entries bearing
stretchers, mangled corpses of family men.
He'd rushed to the vast black cavity of Macbeth
Mine that day, stood among the town waiting.

They'd remain long, dark days, edge
the mine's mouth while rain poured down,
a town of immobile kin. The mournful
cable whine brought them to the surface

body after body

but the screams of widows rising
at each man's recognition haunt
my father still. "It's all we knew."
He shrugged his burly shoulders, pointed

his eyes downward when I made
medical school my goal instead
of coal. "It's over,"
her voice fell flatly in the room.

Cards fluttered to the floor
while I sat, eyes down understanding
that the only life I'd saved
by breaking the chain was mine.

Christine Orchanian Adler

A Railroad

A railroad runs through my life
dirty tracks remind me
this is no earthly garden of eden

A hollow tunnel carves my veins
and before I cross the river
I have to cross the tracks.

T. Paige Dalporto

(*It's Still a Wonder Just Being Here:
Photographs and Poems,* 1999)

Breakfast in West Virginia

Daylight at the end of the street.
The trees are tipped with it.
Oatmeal in a yellow bowl. The roar
deep within the snow drifting along the fence.
Seven words for winter blend softly
in the mouth of the wind.
Cut back the roses. Cedar mulch
on the deep daffodils, deeper tulips.
Avenues along the river, the frozen verge,
barge shadows, old voices trapped
in the capped mines. Seven sounds for coal
piled by the tracks, heaped in open
box cars, furred with frost. A box
of cereal and an empty bowl. Peeled
apple for Phoebe. Walt pours his own milk.
He wants to throw his toast in the snow,
"where the deer can find it." He has his face
against the window, can see the stain
of house lights on the dark yard, the last
stars in the western sky. A car door
slams, the paper hitting the porch. And then
nothing, as the children chew silently, snow
filling slowly every opening in the earth.

James Harms

(*Rivendale* {review}, 2006)

Magnetic Field

You wear magnets around your body.
Like an ancient navigator,
you feel the pull
from icecaps
and point home.

I come to your house beside the creek
just off the Turnpike,
entering through the basement where your husband
drinks J&B all Sunday afternoon
and plays his electric guitar
to the spinning dryer.
"He usually chooses to sleep in the basement," you tell me.

Why do sharp, flashing-eyed women
nurture men who treat them like servants
and spend their days spearing shadows?

I look at the creek, orange with run-off
from "capped" mines,
ski resort aloof above all.

You show me a color-coded
geological map of West Virginia.
"They carried the magnets out with the coal.
We don't have the fields
to energize our bodies.
I'm tired.
We are remnants
short on love."

You give me a book about Buddha.
His birth, enlightenment and death,
unfolded among trees.
Indra lay a necklace across the heavens
so the light of the cosmos
could besparkle our night.

Opening your pouch of jewels,
you lay a magnet in my hand.

Rob Merritt

IV

Life after the Mines

Finished with the Poetry of Coal

Too long, now
trail of ashes
from my grandfather's grave.
I will not wander back
along the broken ties and ballast
leading to the Mingo Roadhouse
where he stoked his locomotives.

I will not think of coal train brakemen
weeping in the chemical dark
of Weirton,
nor of Hambone McCarthy
who came to my grandmother's funeral
almost crazy.

I will not think
of the deep connections of fire
that scarred me
even before I had grown into pain.
I will climb into light
that shines on the earth before me,
my body shedding its grit
of anger and cinders.

Even death has its ending:

let me vine a new brier,
tough over blackened land.

Dick Hague

(*Hard Country*, Bottom Dog Press, 2003)

Unemployment in the Coal Mine Industry

(photo in *Master Photographs*, Paul Schutzer, 1959)

My morning paper route will soon be done forever
   and all these ghost porches of company houses
can go on breathing up the valley air alone.
   Their white painted sides as faded as the snow
falling across the road a flake at a time
   till everything is covered with quiet.
We too are moving on, back home to grandma's
   where the trees are still too thick to climb
and school's an hour away by bus at dawn,
   and the rides there are as dark and deep
as the lines in Daddy's face.

Larry Smith

(*Pine Mountain Sand & Gravel* {review}, 1997)

Tired and Going Home

I can see her as I have seen them all
drooped like a wet rag, turned in tight twists
smoothed then hung out to dry
will be used again
her skin is the deep olive brown mud of the creek
where waters run slow like tired perspiration
rounding down stone stern cheeks

I see her as I have seen them all
lift brown faces to hot blue skies
that burn away the day of scrubbing
the rich lady's house, never complaining
of working too hard, keeping two homes
in just one day, for she's a righteous woman
padding a coal-miner's pay

I see her as I see them all
eyes closed in humble ceremony
praying for the day when aching bones
simply mean growing old
and in her prayer I hear a near silent song
rising up in many tongues
singing from down deep
rhythms about going home

I hear her echo as I have heard
all the echoes of yellow
brown, black women
women yellow-brown
brown-black blue-black women
I hear them say
say someday I'm going down home

home I thought was Virginia or Alabama
maybe Carolina, Louisiana
but when I see the mud in their skin
Georgia's red dust
I know to the earth they all must return
To be used again

Sheila L. Carter-Jones

(*Pittsburgh Quarterly*, 1994)

3 A.M. Train

the whistle blows
on the 3 a.m. train
and stops at the graveyard

it seems as though
the railroad cars
are loading up souls
along with the coal

Souls of dead miners
that owe their essence
to that life-giving cinder

the consistency and cadence
in the wheels carry
the long
distant
hollowing
flute-like bellow
and show me the shame
that isn't mine
but my father's
and his father before him.

an uncle killed
from clearing out
that dead black coal.
and I close my eyes
and see his corpse
loaded onto his
destiny.

Gail Amburgey

(We're Alright But We Ain't Special, co-authored
with Mary Joan Coleman and Pauletta Hansel,
Mountain Union Books, 1976)

Song of Terry

I read somewhere that
the whole damn camp's
for sale.
The old tipple,
jutting like a parapet
near the rim of the Gorge,
the old frame houses
bunched up against the cliffs,
the rotting old company store
with its shitload of garbage
flowing down the riverbank
in back.
Maybe even the old people,
sitting on the porches.
Across a bend in the river
is a wide piece of level land
still owned by the Government,
with nothing on it
but the foundations
of an army training camp.
If I had the money
I'd buy Terry
and move it over there.

P.J. Laska

(*Mucked*, edited by Bob Henry Baber
and Jim Webb, Hesperus Press, 1978)

Hell-for-Certain, Kentucky

> Oh, do not ask, "What is it?"
> Let us go and make our visit.
> —T.S. Eliot
> "The Love Song of J. Alfred Prufrock"

On your way to collect a pension check
in Neon or from that other p.o. box in Whitesburg
your meager need sends you to, the need not to be beholding
to another human being, you detour for a cold drink.
A spring in Ohio and even the crows in Hell-for-Certain
sing "Amazing Grace," or so you say, looping from a night
without sleep on a Greyhound bus. And here you are,
fifty or so miles off the beaten track, sweating in the July sun
before air-conditioning, swiveling around on a fountain bar stool
to catch the attention of a waitress popping her Beeman's gum
as she steps around you, order pad in hand, on her way elsewhere.
Her hair isn't gray-white like yours, though it's pinned back
and twisted in a tight bun as black as your Samsonite suitcase.

Honey, you say, *two Co-colas*. Because I'm there too, beside you,
five, six, and you don't mean to let anyone be so rude
thinking either you're old or not from around here.
But it's no good. She's locked on to the cabbie brought you,
who holds his Pall Mall like an over-the-hill James Dean:
like the next drag of his cigarette will send him somewhere exotic
and maybe she could go, too.

You smile again, and her white uniformed presence spins,
looks you dead in the eyes as if to ask *Bitch, what the hell is it?*
while the Seeburg hi-fi speakers at the counter spew
an Everly Brothers tune. Outside a wall-of-window plate glass
a coal truck grinds its gears, coughing to a stop at the pumps
as if a good case of black lung commenced with inbreathing
all that kicked-up dust from the unpaved state route—

there's always a spark of recognition in a memory like this,
and you'd curse at the busty waitress if it would do any good
or I wasn't on the next bar stool, clutching a Teddy bear
I'll mislay later on the steps of the Letcher County Courthouse.

Roy Bentley

Mine Settlement

Overnight, windows stuck fast,
doors would not close and hung half-opened
on bedrooms, cellar steps, furnace room.
The whole house shifted, went off plumb.
The Bible leaned off its shelf, water spilled
from saucers beneath my mother's African violets.
We walked with one foot lower, while my father
worked along the east foundation, setting up
the half dozen heavy jacks he raised slowly,
one turn at a time. Three days it took
for doors and windows to click shut,
another to lay in new concrete supports,
then the jacks were wound down, the house creaking
and shuddering. For a week we walked gently,
almost whispered to each other. We remembered
the woman hanging clothes who vanished
into the earth. No one slammed a door.
My father rolled a marble over the kitchen linoleum,
all of us happy when it did not roll back.
Nor did we name the abandoned tunnels beneath us,
their rotting timbers, drip of acid water and gas
dissolving the edges of what we most believed.

Harry Humes

(*The Bottomland*, University of Arkansas Press, 1995)

Faced with Starvation, Who Wouldn't Want to Say, Check the Oil and Fill 'er Up?

Kentuckians may not have known the road
but they had jalopies. They didn't care what factory
they landed in. They trailered a perfectly swaying dream
of fair-wage futures, houses with postage-stamp yards
where they might garden. They got the job. After work,
beer bottles fell in dangerous bars with names like Rustic Inn
and the Hide-out. No heart was left unmauled, no face
unmarked by claw swipes from foremen. It wasn't enough
that they worked all the offered overtime; they had to be
punished further with new names like *Briar Hopper*
and *Hillbilly*, pride a payday fat wallet and Coupe DeVille
with white-sidewalled Firestone tires. They courted
their kind in Northern dancehalls; they laughed too loud
at words like *reckon* and *yonder* from voices owned them
lock stock and barrel irrespective of breast size or looks,
no trick of the night the depth of such connectedness,
still another case of the cast-off immigrant
being taught the lessons of landlessness.

Had some whiff of coal smoke tamed them so utterly
that they were persuaded Happiness wasn't a full belly
but a state of mind situated south of the Ohio River?
They might have made it out of poverty,
but among the battlefield casualties of want
was blood, and so they bandaged only their own kind,
did their brand of recruiting and drafting, bragging
of being MIA in an unrecognizable America.
If they were prisoners, so were offspring: a homeland
wasn't what they fought for but moments of belonging
and secular blessing in which bankers didn't ask questions
having to do with their ability to save so much of nothing.
They might clear land of trees that toppled like towers.
so what if they died heartbroken, too young even
to have finished paying for the Cadillac in the drive.

Roy Bentley

The Coal Field Passage

From Winona, once a town
    at the head of Keeney's Creek,
past the stone columned building, once a bank,
and past the houses of the camp long since
    abandoned,
a track bed stripped of tie and rail
switchbacks down the wall of the gorge.
A branch line pulled by corporate decision
    and the sheer weight of taxes
left this one lane trail of rock and sand
where we descend, four in a jeep, laughing
through tunnels the colors of autumn
    to the main line of the C&O
along a hundred million years of river run.
Our guide leaves off his old jokes and reads
    this history from a book:

    The celebration of the line was
    celebrated on January 2, 1873,
    at Hawk's Next. In that same
    year Joseph Lawton Beury's small
    mine at Quinnimont shipped the
    first coal from the New River Field.

The book passed around, and the dusty photographs
    let us in briefly
to see the air heavy with soot and the timber
clear cut to the naked cliff walls.
    And we see how
in the history of industry Beury's memory
    is fixed in stone
at Quinnimont overlooking the rapids.

Here in the river camps nothing remains
except these houses in the shadow of the cliffs
      and pilings of a footbridge
that crossed the river to the Red Ash Mine.

      On September 8, a railroad construction
      crew blasted the sandstones cliffs on the south
      side of the New River, opposite Thurmond. When the
      smoke cleared, there was a perfect profile of
      President McKinley formed on the cliff. The
      startled laborers, mostly Italian, fell to
      their knees, crossed themselves, and cried,
      "Holy Mother!" That afternoon word was received
      in Thurmond that the President had been shot
      in Buffalo, New York.

      "What's that up ahead?"
"Looks like someone walking on the tracks."
      We follow our guide
as the noon sun beats the distant rails
to rubbery incandescence We come upon
the beehive cooking ovens' crumbling brick.
      "People lived in them
in the thirties, whole families. Saw one even
had a piano in it."
      Off in the distance,
an old woman watches us, them moves on slowly,
a larger bundle on her back.
      "Who is she?"
      "What's she doing there?"
"It's Melsina. She's just goin down to Thurmond.
Carries all her belongings on her back. She
worked in the old Beury mansion. Stayed on there
by herself when they closed it up. Train crews

look out for her. Sometimes you see her carrying
an old stray dog like a baby."
We watch her movement fade into the haze
        toward Thurmond,
Believe it or Not City, three times in Ripley,
the town with a railroad for main street.
        "Not much there now."

We turn back, walking north, listening
        to its tales.
". . . had the finest hotels, and I can remember
the bar, the whiskey stacked behind the bar,
and the big one dollar slot machines giving
        them silver dollars,
and the gambling tables lined with velvet . . ."
We pass under the old Nuttalburg coal conveyor—
"I seen five thousand dollars change hands
        in a game of poker . . . "
coming off the cliffs five hundred feet up.
" . . . professionals coming in from the cities is
        what finally broke it up."
        Still owned by Henry Ford.
"First steel tipple on New River," our guide says.
Now rusting away, wooden steps already gone,
        no way up to the controls.
"Shut down after the war and left it all."
The miners recycled the rest of the camp, took
the architecture elsewhere for re-use.
        "Look at this!"
[at the stone foundations of the camp church]
"The operators would always build a church,
to have a place to give the dead miners
        a funeral in."
"Yes, and what about the preachers? There never
was a shortage of preachers."

"You've heard about Yellow Dog, Pete?"
We head back for the jeep, at Caperton camp.
"I seen it up into effect, there
           across the river—
old man Collins brought in Baldwin-Felts men;
           they put a machine gun
           and a search light
on the tipple overlooking the camp."
           At Caperton
we rest on the steps of a big double house,
admiring the carpenter's work, everything
           done by hand,
neatly trimmed, a little something extra for
           the section bosses.
Here the tipple is gone, no sign of the mine.
One question leads to another, and one exclaims,
           "Low coal! Lord,
I loaded coal in nineteen inches, where you had
           to lay on your side,
and if you had a little lump like that, you had
to beat it up before you could get it
           into your car."

And what follows is talk of pickwork and scabwork
and fixing track and being blackballed with
           the Union in '21.
How you had to be as strong as a bristleback,
and our guide says, yes, he worked with a fellow
that had one arm off, had just a short stub,
           call him "Wing,"
one of the best coal loaders that there was.
And play the piano, why after meetings they
           would ask him
and Wing would take that stub and hit the bass
notes and rock back and forth and make the best
           bass run you ever heard.

And he had a by-word, he'd say, "John Brown."
He'd say, "John Brown, I love workin'."
      And yarns spin
until the dead and scattered faces that lived
here once call in a rush of memory that
      leaves us restless,
and standing we see houses, no more than
rotting shells on the hill behind us,
the warm sun softening their sunken roofs.

      "An old man lived
here for a while on Social Security checks."
We walk past a shack on a carpet of lilies
      growing in the yard.
Brick chimney torn down, rusting washbuckets
strewn about, and what must have been his
bed frame and springs outside the door,
      as though
he'd spent the last night under the stars.
      Then in the jeep,
grinding the trail back across trestles of steel
      over waterfalls,
past thick stone walls, laid by hand, following
      the switchbacks,
old railroad warning ropes still hanging,
to the miserable remains of life at the rim,
      the hollow there
a rut filled with cans, bottles and old tires,
the unpainted houses a story of discipline and
      a generation's pain,
of an extraction that gave next to nothing
in return—here a serenity of decay
in wilderness which comes back lush
and strangles what remains like a tourniquet
      on a wound.

We drive home in silence, recalling
the labor of the dead, coal fires
that burned at night, and the rubble left behind.

      P.J. Laska

(*Wages and Dreams*, 1980)

The Day the X-Man Came

I lived in my house
  for 33 years
Before the flood came,
   before the land let loose its
                       tears.
I thought that if you worked
  hard 33 years, well
then just 12 more
  and you could sit and rest
               a spell.

Why,
    I remember one corner of
              the house
      was leanen and fallen in
      33 years ago.
        When my old man came
             haulen in
      wood and blocks and we
              set in
to builden year by year,
      builden what we never had
             before.

It was slow, hard to see
  any end to the builden
       and hammeren,
          but
We saved that corner, built
         it back—
laid away and saved and
       raised five more
    to lay away and save.

All our lives
We ain't never missed a day
  of payen some way,
Doing the best we can,
      But I'm 53 and
      He's 62
      And it's way too late for them
           E-Z credit plans

        Carpet, couch, the family
                tree,
        Baby shoes and Bible too
        Went floaten on down to
           Kermit and Crum
        Floaten away to Kingdom
              Come.

And I know they
      Ain't no amount of misery
      Gonna bring them sweet
           things
    Back to me
And I know it, I know it, I
        know it

But I still can't see
Why we gotta pay
Them Judas strippers to
         haul us away.

How on earth can we
           stand
  Selling our land
     On the installment plan?

And all them politicians that
                    never do
    nothing but pat me on the
                    back
    and tell a lie or two.
Later or sooner, it's all
                    overdue
them floods garnisheed
                    me
they'll garnishee you.

Well, it took all of them years,
  All 33,
    Floods and floods and barrels
                    of tears
    To bring me to this day
And I sit and I cry and I wail
                    and I moan.
        But no amount of hurt and
                    pain's
            gonna float me back my
                    home.

So I just sit and wait
  for the X-Man to come
            burn my builden down

            Not much else to say
            33 years
            washed away

                    Jim Webb

(*Mucked*, edited by Bob Henry Baber
and Jim Webb, Hesperus Press, 1978/1984)

Somewhere Over the Rhine

Left
The homeland of the ragged hills
Left
Their souls hanging on the locust gate posts
Pointed
Weary faces North
Hungry babies sucking bottles
Saw
Blurs of Bluegrass fences
Old cars rattled and smoked
Wheezed
By Sequoia and Dogpatch
Paused
Under the apron at the singular grocery
For peaches and Graham crackers
Glimpsed
"Real live" Indians in vinyl headdresses
Peered
With ashen gray faces out the dusty side windows
Toward the momentary conversations.

Cast
blinks at the Burma Shave signs
Leaned
Into the curves between Lexington and Cynthiana
Headed
To the promised land,
Somewhere over the Rhine.

Fed
The ancient brick houses life
Gave
Light to the midnight air
Noise to the day lit streets.

Had
Dreams in the mind
Pierced by the sirens
Dulled
By the ritual
Pulled
By the absent soul
Left hanging on the Locust gate post.
Late
In the belly of this organism
Searched
For the runway out
Thought
Of the homeland
Left
In the ragged hills.

James Goode

(*Up From the Mines*, Jesse Stuart Foundation, 1993)

excerpt from
From America: A Poem in Process

Lexington, Kentucky

I wish I was a horse
had me a groom
a stable boy a jockey
and a master starve himself
to buy me hay
I wish I was a horse
had me plantations full of grass
for grazing and a swimming pool
and one helluva pretty city
upside down to watch me race
some other horse
every now and then

I wish I was a horse
couldn't read about nothing
couldn't read about some local boy
the daily papers
said they asked him what kind of school he'd
like
the boy said he'd "rather just
be hit by a truck" what
kind of a fool boy is that
in Lexington Kentucky
there's a railroad crossing
holds down traffic to a lengthy idle
while
the coal cars trundle through
The Burlington Northern
coal cars weighing 200,000 pounds each

coal cars carrying its weight again 200,000 pounds
of coal: I reckon takes good track to carry that
a heavy rail
I hear they throw on up to three of them high-
powered engines each one 450,000 pounds at 3/4 of a million
dollars each to pull 100 coal cars taking the goodies
out of Eastern Kentucky
where the only respite for the two-legged
variety of inhabitant is serious or fatal
injury
where
in relationship to The Red River North and The Red
Lake River flowing North
am I
too small
to change anything at all?

June Jordan

(*Working Classics*, edited by Peter Oresick and
Nicholas Coles, University of Illinois Press, 1990)

Another Shoot-Em-Up on the Drive-In Screen

When I saw a cowboy smiling like that
slouching in the line of fire as if invincible
both hands at his side drawling out

"Go for it" across a sea of car hoods
I'd think of my dead uncles who fought
to live after they were fatally shot

I'd memorized details of tavern brawls
because I'd only known them as Story
never as men I'd imagine shaft-mine

private hells private struggles to breathe
I'd vision them pay-day roaring drunk
whispering lies to a lipsticked woman

I'd wonder what it would be like to know
in a breathless instant that not all fist fights
end like a Hollywood western Of course

they had names Ed and Earl and Charlie
and above-ground dreams a lover or two
with glittering earrings and a fondness

for those drowning in the awful facts
of being a coal miner Was it too much
to ask that they not all die of want

Beautiful dreamers was it a shock
taking a bullet like a son of John Wayne
then not being able to walk it off

                    Roy Bentley

Grinning Boy

I am not sure of this at all
but they say along route 2 in West Virginia
where the thin road hugs the wide river
and the air is so full of animals that it smells
like old coffee, a coal miner's wife gave birth
to a grinning boy; a boy with the lips
of Lucifer himself, cursed into never having a bad day
or anything at all to frown about.
They say he'll never grow old.

At night on the western ledge, a cloud hangs
low as the dark grass and rain shoots down like crows'
wings, hard, breaking mirrors and killing cows.
They say it isn't always the rain. I once rode with a man
from Wayne to Point Pleasant, and the river swelled
like a sore finger, pointing us on, shaking
in a soaked wind. Yes, he knew of the miner's wife
but only grinned when I asked about the boy.

I am sure of this:
twelve years I've looked for a right moment,
for a crack in the ground shaped like America,
deep, and not hard to trace. If I find it,
I'll finger the border, stroke Maine like a dog's head,
squeeze Florida like a man,
slide down California without fault.
But my eyes must pretend West Virginia.
Its bones follow mine to a hole in the earth,
this cavern full of coal and lore, this heart
where devils suck air, where boys tread age
like water.

Pamela Steed Hill

(*In Praise of Motels*, Blair Mountain Press, 1999)

Beltline Lights

All the towns die in spite of us.
The coal pours out and out again
like forty years ago and forty before
and the mountains, such a large place,
holding so much back from us.
The mine. Such a small place. Like
constellations in the morning sky the
beltline lights shape our mythologies.

                    Jason Frye

Augury

On the side of the barn—
right in broad daylight—
a luna moth
flattens its phosphorescent self
against a gray oak plank.
It shines—stopping a summer day
in mid-flight—
so bright
it makes me recall
not-so-far-away coal towns,

where moths evolve into colors
closer and closer

to the color of soot.

Eddy Pendarvis

(*Like the Mountains of China*, Blair Mountain
Press, 2003)

The Killin'

For R.T. and all those miners like him

They're gray,
the house, the car,
the flowers in our yard,
all gray.

Sometime after while
the sun'll come up
over the mountains
and slice the dirty fog.

Our noses burn.
Our eyes sting.
At night we cough and wheeze
and a body's hair is never clean.

Yesterday,
Daddy said, "This here killin'
is how we make our livin'.
These dark holes
light the nation."

We buried him this morning.

Wanda Campbell

(*Rogue Scholars* {review}, 2005)

The Mountains Have Numbers

they tell me in Logan.
   When the sun rises
or sets behind those hills,
   you don't think Blair Mountain,
you think six or 26.

   And that if you grew up in a mining camp,
you learned those numbers
   like breathing,
along with the days of the week
   and how to tell time.

They tell me that even now,
   though most of the mines are boarded up,
directions are still given in numbers,
   not mountains:
"You go past Holden 22.

   If you pass Hewitt Creek,
you've gone too far."

Laura Treacy Bentley

Quaintness in WV

 In winter everything is the color
of a stick or a gopher. These
quiltless hills become the bed
of a restless sleeper under
a frayed blanket.

The planes that cross above the humps,
from Cincinnati, Pittsburgh,
and faraway Atlanta
carry passengers who look down
thinking of a bed full of cousins.

But down here it's mostly winter,
stick-brown groundhogs,
and days of ball bearing skies.
Here we can do almost
anything, just not very well.

If you want real skill, real sky, real
groundhogs, go north or east, where
the mine owners live, where the bigger
beds are, where it's flat enough
for full-grown jets to land.

                    Ron Houchin

Classical Influences and Economic Recovery
Up Thornton Creek in Letcher County

Before I learn about
marble remnants
strewn across Aegean isles
I learn about
abandoned tipples
where they flank iron rails
ratcheting the hollow
tie by tie,
rails servicing
increasingly efficient
preparation plants.
Instead of
fallen temple columns,
I see collapsing coal chutes
draping slagged slopes
with corrugated rust.

Stone foundations
left to ruin
across the creek behind
our camp-row house
imbue me with the same respect
Greek pillars
must evoke for
pre-Pearl Harbor travelers
deliberately seeking
visceral pull of
manmade monuments not
clawing at
Earth's crust
to stay in place

but plunging tentacles
to strata deep as
despot horrors long compressed
and dark as unleashed tyrants'
pitch-black
hardened hearts.

Without instruction
I am not without ability
to understand how
an edifice becomes more than it is
by connecting the beholder
to unseen forces,
how booming enterprise can
portend dissolution
dire as thwarted productivity.

I am a mountain coal camp child
shielded from deprivation
during the Great Depression,
not shielded from
unnamed apprehension
tumbling off recovery's
rolling tonnage heaped too high.
Later I will realize
how classic tragedy unearthed
in seven glorious Limnos layers
is faintly echoed here
in hills where ever-deeper seams
are plumbed for reasons
not apparent to the
ones who toil.

The working tipple's
out of sight
on up the hollow

toward the schoolhouse
and road's end.
Sometimes the long
conveyor belts keep rumbling
like the sounds of war
throughout the night.
Uneasy in our sheltered beds
we stir, our dreams propelled by
glistening loads of promise
gliding by
toward destiny as dubious
as ancient cargo
on the way
to Peloponnesian
ports.

Marietta Ball

A Diffident Heaven

Spring storms plate the walls
pewter, affixing the metals
of light. Place domineers here:
it fates the qualities of light
as the hierarch tiers of mountain slate
dictate the difficult winding roads
coal trucks gouge and pleat.

Tuesday, I drove past three shanties
built of plastic, ply board, and tin
foundered on a ridge too thin
for houses. Blue tarps
mended one, lending it
a gaiety that hurt.
The store nearby was taciturn:
"Junk," it said, and spurned
nothing—hats, washers, doors.
The latter were up-ended in rows
like books pressing the airs
of the abandoned rooms
between them. A barn beside it
of corrugated tin said
in faded black and gold,
Chew Mail Pouch Tobacco.

Further on, a half-mile long coke plant
sported flumes—flame panted
from two thirty-foot stacks.
The off-ramp sign said
Belle. The river pleated
and dimpled with light beyond it.

Still, native violets
and dandelions cohabit
on lawns and rural road-cuts:

purple and yellow, yin and yang,
clash and complement—
signs of the land's contrary
powers. All night, Spring storms worry
the native dogwood, whose
rust-pink flowers don't appear
in the field guide.

The four petals, thumb-wide,
waxy and thick, rust-notched
at each tip, shade to ivory
then peridot at the calyx.
Each cups its seed in clutches
of green buck-shot. The notched
petals form a cross-Celtic—
the rust stains like stigmata
warn and mourn.

We heard too as we drove
West Virginia's almost heaven
the seventy kinds of singing birds
Copeland evokes.
The narrow hills were
tufted with trees
just leafing out, barely furred,
chartreuse and blurrily
immature
like young men's beards,
yet aged too, like old men's skulls,
sparsely whiskered, hairs
spooked erect by a scare.

Underneath, a buried
hub of machinery hums—
a diffident heaven's factory.

                    Mary Moore

Backlash on the West Virginia Line

Every shining pine needle, every sandy shore, every mist
in the dark woods, every meadow, every humming insect.
All are holy in the memory and experience of my people.

What befalls the earth befalls all of the sons of the earth.
Chief Seattle

I hear land speaking.
Rhododendron bushes descant with murmur of Wolf Creek
when I kneel beside the trail,
but more often
it cries for retribution
from the hills.

McDowell County, West Virginia:
those who stayed when the mining companies left—
blasted by summer deluges.
Cleaned up and rebuilt,
then April flood.
Landgraff washed over the edge.
Not one building left.
Where do the people go?

Bluefield:
Breast cancer.
Colon cancer.
I hear "chemotherapy" every day.
People I drank beer with:
a photographer who caught the glint off
the ruined roadhouse atop East River mountain,
a woman who knitted skullcaps for hairless patients.
Good people caught in the backlash.

Perpetrators have escaped, live in Pittsburgh.
Those who stay because of no money or love of that earth
caught in land's fury.

Cherokee say when a horrible event occurs in a place—rape, murder—
dirt and trees hold that violence.
Hikers feel a chill.
European settlers said "haunted."

My neighbor, a coal company lawyer,
tells me there have been floods since Noah,
as his company rips landholding trees
from the mountainsides.

The land is screaming to be heard
from a seam running square through Bluefield, West Virginia,
where in one family of four children:
one dead of breast cancer,
one dead of colon cancer,
one with a metal plate in her head
where a brain tumor was removed.

Other mountain communities,
like the grass-covered hills of Grayson Highlands
where there was no mining,
don't kill people.

I hear a man cursing a woman a few streets over.
Teenagers vandalize libraries.
Churches burn.
Wounded wound back.

A ravaged mountain crushes soul
as well as body, but still we must try to listen
to what still grows—the herbs
and the spirits

that can unhaunt places
where human and nonhuman cohere.
I look at the sun through the rhododendron
as I hike beside Little Wolf Creek.

I greet others who share the camaraderie
of the forest. Like Job, we discover
> *The birds of the sky, they will tell you,*
> *Or speak to the earth, it will teach you;*
> *The fish of the sea, they will inform you,*
and by each of us restoring our sliver of landscape
we are praying.

Rob Merritt

An Old Coal Tipple
(unchained)

Weathered beams groan like a young miner's moan
when, too early, he
has to rise, or
too early he
dies.
Loose, rusted tin
screams out in the wind,
(or was that the widow
of a long lost friend?)
The crossties beneath are soft with rot
like the miners we forgot
who suffered slow death
from lack of breath—
black lung, or just a myth?
Now there's no more coal cars weighing that hard load,
there's no more black cars on that long, slow road.
Tomorrow this tipple will fall to the track,
and their sorrow, when my people look back
will make them stronger for the task at hand
for they no longer
are chained to this land.

Kenneth Donald Haynes

(*Appalachian Heritage,* Summer 2006)

Sketches from Appalachia

underground miner
"shoots the coal"
the fog of dust
to breathe in
breathe out

setting
the jack
a roof bolter
with "safety first"
taped to his helmet

by drills and cuts
the continuous miner
shrinks the space
between worker
and machine

battery pack belts
never returned
a check at the lamp house
for the brass tags
of those still missing

hazy sunlight
makes its way down
the appalachians
an eerie reflection
in the slurry
the sulphur smell
near a tumble-down
mountain
no one is sure
how long slag will burn

abandoned tipple
a barefoot boy
contemplates
the world
with folded arms

Cindy Tebo

V

Environmental Degradation

Coal Fern

The green ferns that lift from the forest's damp floor
Grow full in the autumn and scatter their spore;
The white ferns that silver the frost of the glass
At midnight will come and at morning will pass.

But the black fern that lies in the coal's hidden seams
Still treasures the quantum's primordial streams
From the sun of the lost suns that died long ago
When the dinosaur quaked on the edge of the snow,
And the great pterodactyl's reptilian flight
Sent down on the fern-trees the shadow of night.

Then the great silent fern-trees in darkness decayed
And treasured and measured and captured and laid
The core of the atom in infinite shade.

Louise McNeill

(*Elderberry Flood*, Elderberry Books, 1979)

The Age of Optimism

In 550 BC, Herostratus,
hungry for fame, and
begging the world
to remember his name,
burned to the ground
the Holy Temple of Artemis.
We can hardly imagine
one of the seven marvels of the world,
destroyed by a madman's cravings!

The citizens of Ephesus
would never recover from their despair
yet, human spirit being what it is,
rebuilt the structure
in 356 BC.
And with it erected
a law stronger than marble,
more enduring than gold:
Anyone who would mention

the name or utter the word
Herostratus shall be put to death,
and so some were.
Historians tell us
that no act of destruction,
can be imagined
(. . . *even, they said, the burning of the*
New York Stock Exchange,
as preposterous, as unlikely,
as that event might seem. . .)

no deed of lunacy
would ever again

wreak the horror of the
destruction
of Diana's holy place
in history,
no grief
could ever match that
of the Ephesians.

Now imagine
the natural marvels of our world
destroyed by
human greed.
There is no single name to put to death.
There is no grief like that
which mourns the loss of mountains,
temples that cannot be restored
not even with miracles
not even with marble and gold.

Grace Cavalieri

Song of Destiny

Here is my song of destiny I sing,
Not that I crave the blood of any man,
To take his life and doom him in his spring!
But here he comes and takes my people's life.
He takes their earnings made by blood and sweat,
He cuts the trees from my Kentucky hills,
He digs the coal from my Kentucky mines—
And even cuts for pleasure our small pines.
And do I sing, my friend, for any man
Who preys upon us like we're suckling lambs?
And I am tired of prayer and wished "God damns."
It is the time this folly comes to end
As summer grass comes to an end by frost.
These trees are friends of mine and yet they die,
Their stumps stand under blue moons like thin ghosts,
They leave such emptiness beneath the sky.

Jesse Stuart

(*Songs of a Mountain Plowman*, Jesse
Stuart Foundation, 1931/1986)

The Brier's Pictorial History of the Mountains

Green wilderness rolling like an ocean.
Moccasins moving along a buffalo trail.
Deer slip down to a salt lick in the evening.

A shot. Another and another. A wolf wheels
on a mountain path, turned by the smell of gunsmoke.

The creak of wagon wheels. A baby cries.
Axes ring in the woods. A cabin rises
in the circle of sunlight living in a clearing.

Green trees pale before deadening axes.
The woods fall back, heading for high ground.
Fields follow, pushing the woods uphill,
taking all the ground up to the rib rock.

Lights burn in houses at the mouths of creeks,
in cabins up the coves. School bells.
Laughter of children on the road to school.
A fiddle tune, a dance, stories, songs
that still remember the Scottish border, the English
towns, the great halls, and the ocean.

Timber crews move across the ridges.
Rafted logs ride out on April floods.
A locomotive pushes through the trees,
following the paths of the first wagons.
A Model-T rolls through a mountain town.
A farmer leans his hoe against a stump,
another unhitches a gray horse forom a plow
left standing in a thin-soiled, gullied field
his grandfather plowed when it was newground.

Radios start talking in the leaves.
Coves and hollows empty toward coal camps.
Men go underground. In coves and hollows,
a plow point on a rock pile; a horsehair hanging
on a staggering barbed-wire fence.
A cabin leans and drifts. A spring and spring drain
choke on fallen leaves. Fields grown old
and tired give ground back to a generation
of woods returning to claim them. A panther screams.

White-eyed miners ride out of the shafts
to meet the match of any hundred miners:
a D-9 dozer roots along a ridge,
finds the black vein and takes it from the top.

Now coal camps where ten thousand lived before
sink in on themselves like cabins in the coves,
and like old fields, give up to the woods.
A concrete sidewalk running beside a creek
pitches, breaks; weeds grow out of the cracks.
Smaller walks that turned off and rose,
twelve steps up to a miner's house, rise now
to woods. Squirrels chatter and the creek runs.

Cut up and bleeding, the land lies breathing hard,
in places torn and gouged beyond all healing,
in others beautiful and blessed as ever.

Already scouts from east and west, in search
of water, have looked over the rim of hills.
Like long hunters, they have stayed and seen,
and sent word back to cities, turning the eyes
of millions out in the world toward the mountains.

                              Jim Wayne Miller

        (*Brier, His Book*, Gnomon Press, 1988)

Goliath

(They Can't Put It Back)

for Ewel

Down in the valley 'bout a mile from me
Where the crows no longer cry
There's a great bit earth-moving monster machine
Stands ten stories high
The ground he can eat is a sight
Takes a hundred tons at a bite
He can dig up the grass
It's a fact
But he can't put it back

They come and tell me I got to move
Make way for that big machine
But I ain't movin' unless they kill me
Like they killed the fish in my stream
But look at that big machine go
Took that shady grove a long time to grow
He can rip it out with
One whack
But he can't put it back

I never was one to carry signs
Picket with placards
Walk in lines
Maybe I'm behind the times!

You can bet your sweet life they're gonna hear from me
I ain't gonna take it layin' down
Cause I'm getting' tired seein' rocks that bleed
On the bare guts of the ground

I ain't goin' to sell my soul
So they can strip out another tiny vein of coal
I ain't a-movin' out of my tracks
Cause they can't put it back
THEY CAN'T PUT IT BACK!

Billy Edd Wheeler

(*Song of a Woods Colt*, Droke House, 1969)

Go Tell the Children

Go tell the children the mountain is trembling,
An earth-moving monster is eating its way
Through grapevines and shumate and wild laurel thickets
And even Sweet William has fallen prey.

Go tell the children their true love is dying,
The whippoorwill's song no more shall they know;
Go tell the children to bow down in sorrow;
The fullness of mountains—of mountains must go!

Go tell the children to weep for the passing
Of redbuds and sarvis—a sight to be seen!
Tell them to hang down their heads in their sorrow
As they sing, "Green gravel, the grass is so green."

The flowers of the fringe tree are blacker than midnight,
The blue fruit now lies on the crust of dead earth;
No more shall white flowers hang down like fringes;
O, Go tell the children that I weep at their birth!

Go tell the children that trailing arbutus
Lies in cold ashes of campfires once red,
That pipestem and spicebush now yield to the slaughter;
O, Go tell the children the mountain is dead!

Muriel Miller Dressler

(*Appalachia, My Land*, Morris Harvey College, 1973)

The Execration of Maust
(The Stripping of Cold Knob)

> "Earth is alive. The soil is her flesh,
> the rocks are her bones, the wind is her breath,
> trees and grass are her hair.
> She lives spread out, and we live on her.
> When she moves, we have an earthquake."
> —from an Okanogan Legend.

God's Renegade? Contemporary Neanderthal?
Satan's Blood Brother?
What kind of a man were you, Maust?
How great was the audacity or ignorance
that compelled you to gut Cold Knob—
God's jewel, the beauty,
third highest peak in the state?
What crossed your mind
when your blade turned the first rib up to air,
when the coal, exposed at last,
lay in a heap at your feet?
And when you looked out over your legacy
to the Greenbriar Valley and Virginia
did you feel almost akin to the creator
knowing you had the brute power to wreck
in one short year
what eternity had wrought?

Maust, did the coal light Cleveland
for eleven minutes?
Did you turn a handsome profit
on the hunchback of grief?
Did the boy from Scarsdale laugh all the way
to the Florida bank
when he told the Great State of West Virginia
where it could stick
its $50 an acre Reclamation Bond?

And did your heart ever know guilt or remorse, Maust—
the pang of a man who has screwed mother nature?
Or did you roar off to town
tightening your swashbuckling pants
and bragging of your exploits
all over what was still left of creation
till drunken sleep reclaimed you?

Maust
  did the spirit of trees come then
  to haunt your fitful dreams?
Maust
  did a chorus of ancient rocks
  curse you in the dead of night?

Maust
  did bulldozers strip the skin from your flesh?
Maust
  did men with green eyes rip black guts
  from your chest and leave you to die
  unattended and Canadian cold
  on the side of the Knob
  your pathetic demise frozen
  in the eyes of stoic deers and black bears?

If there is justice in the world, Maust
        they did so
        they did so

    Bob Henry Baber

(*A Picture from Life's Other Side*, 1994)

Cold Knob, Reclaimed

(putting lipstick on a corpse)

From scalped rim the blue ridge stretch
violet mist draped towards Trout Valley
from Kennison Mountain and Bushy Ridge
designated by rustic timber company plaque—

behind our back, in shale at highwall base
the rustic timber company pine-seedlings,
hostages of stupidity,
half-dead issue of our greed,
are now over a quarter century old.

Bob Henry Baber

(*A Picture from Life's Other Side*, 1994)

The Strike

gray snowflakes scud the black
coal
exchange building, miners hug
shaken shoulders shafted
by splinters of sweat-
ed nightmares. rockets implode
47 dead headlines. deadlines.
talks. sklat. talks spelled
backward. the governor he and the union
leader he and he
the management sklat gray.
breadless tables and empty box
cars and black coal
dust wait,
as the gray snowflakes scud
black bituminous irises glint,
red lobes crackle.
the question resonates and the answer is
sklat…the weather bureau forecasts
more global warming.

Mary Lou Pratt

(*The Guyandotte Poets*, edited by Robert Gerke
and Arline R. Thorn, Trillium Press, 1993)

Fissures

November's forest fires are still
Burning this spring—
The mine-break fire,
Under snow
The wet dead leaves
A thin crust of ash,
Suddenly flames out
The mountainside
Is fissured, hollowed
By burning seams of coal
Outcrops glow at night
And sulfur and smoke
Swirl into the dawn
They say the hunter
Not knowing this terrain,
Intent upon the fading track,
Might suddenly break
Through frosty leaves and slide
Down feet-first into hell.

Arline R. Thorn

(*Fire & Ice*, Trillium Press, 1993)

After They Moved the Big Sandy:
Potter's Hill Cemetery, Yeager, Kentucky

That red breast of earth
suckling hoary grandfathers and
sisters who might have been.
That final curtain of soil
drawn over bone and silk
and preference.

That shadowed lump
pocked with carved granite,
marble lambs, crumbling angels,
a tiny sign my mother painted.

That hill has sung *I'll Fly Away*
so many times
it threatens to leave itself,
stripping stone from box,
gravel from clawed hand,
the sand flowing away like time,
leaving only roots.

                    Elaine Bentley Baughn

Transmission Lines

Power's generated here
all along the Ohio
and from the ravaged interior—
the life from the black rock,
fossil sunlight freed,
transformed
into living current.

Likewise my thought
carried over long silver wires,
vibrating grid of words
looping from river to ridge,
hilltop to hilltop
pylon to pylon.

Monuments of energy—
chimney stacks
and cooling towers stand up where
the ransacked work of eons
consumes a lifetime,
obliterates its homestead,
the generations' living, dying.

The residue
deposited in ponds as fly-ash words,
dispersed into the wind as acid tears,
discharged into the stream, emotion cooled.
That burning
transmitted now as light upon this page.

Arline R. Thorn

(*Mining the Seam*, Trillium Press, 1992)

Deep Well, Buffalo Creek

One story warned of water so foul
it writhed underground. We moved in.
Your grandfather owned the land.
Hills once rose over the sun, fell back
to the house. We could look straight
into the tabled water changing color
rust to acid, in the rock. We drank.

We were thirsty. Trains ran out of river
downhill into the mines. When the water
ran uphill, we knew the dam had broken
the company's promise. Another tall story
drowned in denial and a mountain of mud.
We had to keep drinking, keep climbing.
Some fell ill. The rest got stronger.

Art Stringer

(*Riverwind,* Fall 2005)

Rivers

More than just rivers,
They pour their souls into seas,
As troubled patients spill their thoughts
To attentive ears above this world's couches,
In latitudes
Where twin poets
Speed through Draper Valley
On a joy ride to the madhouse.

More than just rivers,
They write metaphors
In a special language of water, sky, and leaves
While sticking tongues into salt water
Like great men carrying their power with them
While reaching for their future,
So fully aware of where they've been.

More than just rivers,
They unfold action
That probes different views of truth.
I read their flow of pages
Toward the skewed Appalachian delta
Void of tulip poplar ridges
Somewhere west of Tiger Tail Beach
Where the gulf lies replete with family farms—
Bull-tongue plows lost beneath silt,
Strip-mined boulders worn to smooth beach pebbles—
Strewn with a legacy of bones,
Male and female joined in a new anatomy—
While a confetti of dead leaves
Drapes river snags
That sing slurred songs
In an absolute oral tradition,
A requiem that cannot be denied.

M. Ray Allen

The Storm*

      She is hesitant to smile.
A holiday created by surprise
        as the wind comes through
        its significant presence.
It is unclear why,
        but she must keep trying.

"We had a community
        but we had to leave."
A cold misty rain that was more felt than seen,
The little creek transformed,
        chasing the residents out of the hollow.
She was not deterred.

Some are in need of a greater comfort factor.
            So you do the math.
            Unite their negotiating power and
make the designs seem animated.
"The first domino has been irrevocably pushed
        over."
She wants to smile,
        it is accessible and visible.
Then she'd say a prayer.
"In reality, it probably won't make much difference
        in what has been a crippling inertia."

While millions tune in
        like maniacs.
It was not immediately known whether anyone was
        injured,
        bits of fog mingled in the trees above.
They (officials responding to the scene)
        determine if their neighborhood is safe.

Which they inaccurately reported.
Both sides are eager to finish.
        Who won this one?
Agents had not kept promises they made.
        We shouldn't conduct business like that.
Economic development continues
        nonetheless.
The incident left visible marks on her neck,
        left the place in a shambles.

They watch as their houses and belongings
        were ruined.
"Someone failed
        to provide better opportunities we didn't
                have in the past."
Someone worked to rebuild a life,
        it was clean and warm.

FEMA put them up in the local Super 8 motel
        surrounding the rows of identical trailers.
All along she
        stays amazingly upbeat
        "at least we're all together in a warm place."
With a little autumn red and yellow,
        but down below there was no color,
save for the trailers against the late November landscape.

Lack of land.
A struggling economy.
Personal financial problems
        forced them to overcome many hurdles
It's the little things that make it tough.
Propensity for falling seems natural.

This is the reality
    the storm has sparked.
Like so many times before,
    true hell descended from the hills above.

Caitlin Cunningham

*This is a found poem composed of phrases in local newspapers in Kanawha County.

from "**Coal Camp Child**"

Things have changed.
I no longer know
where the hollows are,
babbling brooks nor mossy glens
where my childhood secrets are stored.

The pungent smell of coal rising from
mountain seams,
The perfume of wild honeysuckle
and mountain laurel blooms,
Chewing the sweetness of birch barks,
Tasting wild strawberries and persimmons
Quenching my thirst from a hidden spring
my lost elixir. . .

Tainted waters of iron and sulphur
bleed now orange-red
from abandoned mines.

Desolation flows down the mountain sides.

Sarah Cornett-Hagen

Water Cycle Syllabus to Surpass a Coal Camp Course

Metallic, barren water underlined our early
lessons. Deeply deceptive slate-dump
ponds instructed iridescently.
Ditches demonstrated slimed pollution
by refusing to foster tadpoles. After rains swelled
creeks to ropy yellow rush that took
the bridges out, flood-musk lecture lingered
between banks lined with mud-scummed
weeds laid over in postures of
downstream supplication. We lived with daily
warnings to stay away from water.

But our spirits harbored knowledge
of fern-consecrated rills with crystal falls,
of the gurgling song of riffled descent
to clear sandy-bottomed pools
where minnows moved among bright pebbles.
We perceived beyond apparent text
how coal mine run-off was but an imperfection
in the enduring flow. We knew this
sickened, tortured segment
modified to nature's way upstream
and downstream out of sight.

We understood about
sweet springs at heads of hollows
rising in forest loam, about wide rivers'
silent sliding depth, about the ocean's
ancient salty sprawling swing.
We sensed regeneration
in lightening bolt and rising mist.

We knew there was no
beginning and no end, that all waters
were linked together. We knew that water,
however assaulted in its cycle,
was the way.

Marietta Ball

An Ode to Mountaintop Removal

Look, the night
is upon us.
The mountains have come

to darkness
and the last deer has given
itself to the hunter.

The trees are dissolving
into their own shadows.
The trumpet vine

has sounded its final call,
and the tap root
of the honeysuckle is pulling

its last breath of fragrance
from the earth.
The fox has no truck

with the rabbit
and the squirrel in its nest
dozes and twitches

while the bobcat
sharpens its perfect claws.
To have learned anything

in this life is to listen.
Still, no one hears
the blacksnake swallow

the robin's blue egg.
The cricket has ceased
its raspy saw

and there is no whisper
of water
from ephemeral streams,

nor any owl
or whippoorwill calling
in this dark.

                    Charlie Hughes

Black Windows

The word is "potterracking,"
odd Appalachian term,
describing the racket guinea hens make,
or, in this case, a loud gabble-
gaggle of businesswomen
who will not shut up though it's
the last hour before dawn and
everyone else on the plane
is trying to sleep. What fascinates me

is how, mannerless, they seem to live
the narcissistic fantasy I can only dream—
that the planet is theirs alone, that others
exist only as audience, as prop.
How fine it must be to know
everything you say is of interest to everybody.
How excellent to have a mouth that inexhaustible
in a world where, really, there is less and less
of importance to say. More and more,

it is silence I choose, turning towards
black windows in which the mountains,
the last of the night, shift by beneath me.
First, the lights of Charleston, West Virginia,
curving along the Kanawha. Then, as we fly
south towards Charlotte, hills of the coalfields,
and one great gray flatness where machines
have torn off the mountaintop to reach the last
of the coal. The blood of hills is acid, gray
or orange, staining the creek-beds. How often,

within each minute, is someone conceived,
does someone give birth? Down the aisle,
the potterracking mounts, voice layered on voice,

strata of shrieks. Between the mountains,
lights slither along the valleys, promising
to improve paradise, gleaming like phosphorescent
snail trails, radioactive spoor. The mountains themselves,
the mountains that remain, are too steep
for trailer park, automobile dealership, mall.
This distant from dawn, unpeopled,
they are black arching against black.
It is only darkness that gives me hope.

Jeff Mann

Gap

A train hauling Kentucky coal
mounts the Blue Ridge,
vaulting through an unnatural
gap—black men blasted through granite.

From this high knob,
that train hardly appears to be
technology: it's slithering
like a black snake

reigning in a kudzu kingdom,
eating everything
in its path; people can't escape
from its huge mouth,

so they don't try:
they line the track, and the long train
tears down the slope . . . it's a monstrous god
that moves mountains—

if not for them . . .

Ted Olson

Mountain Travesty

They're beheading West Virginia,
Sending her down to New Orleans.
We can make the same trip
Floating on the shallow streams,
Sluice through our downsized mountains
Mortified by flat topped crew cuts,
Summits scalped where oak and pine once stood.
They're moving Appalachia
Peak and pinnacle
Through the slurries in the valleys
Cut between the headless hilltops,
Where she's hemorrhaging
Her "Wild and Wonderful"
While she's stripped of the old claim
To her mountain maiden name,
Someday she'll be reclaimed
As the Appalachian plains
When they finally dislocate
Her crowning glory
Where the gulf winds' sultry blow
Warms the Mississippi delta
And Old Man River
spews his silt
Into the Gulf of Mexico,
Hey, we're sending Appalachia
Down to New Orleans
Filling swamp and marshland
With majestic Mountain grandeur
Near the Louisiana bayou,
Come with me!
We can sit along the shoreline,
Sing about our heritage,
And watch the West Virginia mountains
Sink into the salty sea.

Max Price

Locrian

Where is there to rest?
Not the pasture, where the ground-cherries plumped,

where, in late summer, ironweed pooled.
not the forest, where the flicker hammered,

where we walked among the emerald,
illicit hand in hand, where we sucked nectar

from nipped honeysuckle blooms. Not the loft
of last century's barn, where hay scratched our cheeks

as we lay through the rain, storm strumming
corrugated tin, sipping moonshine from a flask,

beard to beard, post-seminal drowse. Not
the farmhouse porch, or wedding ring quilt, or the pantry full

of canned peaches, corn relish, half-runners.
You left long ago, for another life,

and tonight I am landless, driving these backroads drunk,
snow swirling in the headlights, and what we owned is gone.

Now strangers yank our oaks from the earth.
Tree roots sprawl against the sky. They gasp like landed trout,

stacked shoulder to shoulder, bier-burnt. It is a blessing now, how
you are not here, how you do not see machines break the moss-

stained stones, stain the streams with vermilion, tangerine, puce,
bury the water deep. My grandfather's pasture is a bowl

of shattered shale, the maple grove a heap of boulders,
a clatter of coal trucks. The well is dry, the farmhouse flattened,

the cornfield a great beast's dung-heap, where it scratches up
dust and hides its waste. There is only the graveyard left,

where, each Memorial Day, we trimmed the spruce boughs
and the weeds about the graves, then lay together, naked

inside May, inside young grass and red maple shade.
Once I hoped we might have ended here, this fret where,

after unrelenting dissonance, a callused forefinger slides
into peace, into resolution. Ferrell Ridge, last tooth left

in a shattered mouth. Headstone bearing one name,
not two. I lean against it, pretending it is a mighty tree.

I sip from the pewter flask you bought me in Scotland.
In Celtic swirls, two warriors share a cup.

Tomorrow the blasting and digging will begin again,
rocks fall from the sky, hills upend themselves, but tonight

it is silent enough to hear the chimes of frost, the slow way
ice marries my moustache. I take another swig. I cannot feel my toes.

Tonight I will trace the stars, stroke the few last trees,
Someone must stay to console the dead, name the mountains
          that are gone.

                              Jeff Mann

(*Appalachian Heritage*, Summer 2006)

The Aftermath

from the drenched,
drooping limb
one last wet drop
of rain
falls to break
the mirrored film
on the puddle,
in the lane.

Kenneth Donald Haynes

Nantahala*

Shadows
descend the hills.
Morning light
comes late
to the Blue Ridge.
Along the trails
we hear
this advice:
give to the wounded land,
coiled
and
waiting,
a song
composted
from terror
and pity.

Rob Merritt

*Cherokee for "Land of the Noonday Sun." Sunlight
reaches the valleys of the Appalachian mountains
only when directly overhead at midday. Enlightenment is brief.

234

Abandoned

Sometimes his mind flew black as a crow
over hundreds of coves and hollers
fallen silent since people were swept
out like rafted logs on spring's high water.

Then his life would stand
empty as an abandoned house
in one of those forgotten places,
his days like blackened chimneys
standing in fields going back
to the thickets of second growth—
untended tombstones in a cemetery
up some lost valley.

Sometimes he thought there was nothing left
but the life of a half-wild dog
and the shelter of a junked car
turned on its back in a ditch, half
grown over with honeysuckle.

Or else his life became the house
seen once in a coal camp in Tennessee
the second story blown off in a storm
so stairs led up into the air
and stopped.

                    Jim Wayne Miller

            (*The Mountains Have Come Closer*,
            Appalachian Consortium Press, 1980)

VI

Resistance

The Company

(Coal Miner)

The Company owned the houses,
And The Company owned the store;
The Company paid the Sheriff off,
And fixed the Schoolhouse door.

The Company owned the Baldwin-Felts,
And opened up the bar;
And set the tipple on its stilts,
And lit the Christmas Star.

They owned the mountain and the mine,
The river and its fork;

They summered in the Byzantine
And wintered in New York.

Louise McNeill

(*Elderberry Flood,* Elderberry Books, 1979)

Picket Line

I remember that miner's brains
Lying on a black Kentucky road
After the gunshots died,
Brain cells clustering still,
Reflecting off the pavement.
The hollow-eyed children,
The pock-marked road signs,
The fires going out,
The rancid coffee urns,
The Southern States store
With its windows broken,

Those brains holding secrets that will never be told,
        Love songs still waiting to be sung,
A hankering for shoo-fly pie,
        The names of birds and trees
        And babies unborn, unseeded.

Brains like soft tapioca,
Like cheese not yet ripened,
Waiting for crows, waiting

To sleep, to speak, to sigh, to sing,
To draw one more breath for each of them

Oh, watch where you step.
Look before you leap.
Measure twice before you cut.
Oh, be careful!

                    Barbara Smith

Something of America

A friend once said:
"If you want to be a good patriot
don't read your country's history
too closely. . . ."

But something of America I know
love and cherish
with warm pride
and something I intensely dislike.

The Great Dream
Like the rising of a fair morning
with Thomas Paine
has never been equaled.
But the recording made it
a dream deferred—
left slavery unmentioned
made a Bill of Rights for white men.
Black and red men, women of all
                colors
were omitted . . .

In the hearts of the lowly
Thomas Paine never died.
There no slavery lived
no grabbing of red people's
                homeland.
John Burnett walked the trail
of tears and suffering with the
                Cherokee.
Appalachian-rooted John Fairfield
laid his own life down
on the shadowy underground
of thousands of Black folk
toward freedom.

Numerous unknown headlines
annals of unrecorded history
speak still of justice and peace.
Workers, the humble poor, plain
                people,
producing life substance
plan no battles, make no wars
for blood to drip

that profits may continue
in undiminished flow...

Many I know who now harbor
peace and justice and sharing:
John Woody and Effie
keep hope a-flicker
in desolate Matoaka.
John Woody, a man I know of 48
                years
waiting to die of black-lung,
never knew the school room,
went to the mine at nine.

Effie and the children
robbed of his manhood
grieve silent tears
on the sad Matoaka hills.
But John's courage stands tall,
remembering Blair Mountain,
Cabin and Paint Creeks,
Ludlow and Coal Creek—
years when miners held
union meetings in secret places.

Once at strike time I found
                John's body
unconscious, beaten
on a rutted trace,
Empty coffin, a warning,
was left in his yard
labeled "John Woody" in large
                letters.
When told what the letters said
he smiled.
"That's the last thing I need,"
                he said.

Cabin Creek, alive in heroic tales,
unrecorded.
There Clifton and Mary Bryant
fuel the flame in their humble hut.
Blair Mountain, 1921
Ten thousand miners in struggle

bombs dropping from air.

West Virginia knew Debs—
in Moundsville Prison,
and in 1912 elected fifty-five
of his party to public office!
West Virginia mountaineers
seceding from slavery in 1863
enslaved to corporate power later—
Consolidated, Continental,
Peabody, U. S. Steel,
Rockefeller. . .

And Ludlow—
bitter in memory Ludlow!
Hungry miners
evicted to tent colony
fearing Rockefeller police bullets
dug an under-tent pit
for women and children's safety.
Rockefeller guards drenched and set
        fire.
Thirteen children and a pregnant
        woman
burned to death.
Five men and another woman shot.

O, celebrate the risen Christ
Easter Sunday, 1914
Celebrate the murder of 19 workers!

Ludlow. . .!
Map markers leave it off now.
A stone-carved miner
with wife and slain child at foot
mark the spot to:
". . . the men, women and children
who died in freedom's cause
April 20, 1914."

Ludlow, bitter in memory Ludlow!

And Coal Creek, Tennessee,
blotted, too.
Pleasure-seeking tourists at

"Lake City" don't know
the bitter—and glorious—
story of Coal Creek.
Change the name
blot the memory. . .!

Hope and hurt, blood and terror
lie heavy in Coal Creek memory.
Mountain men there lit the spark
destined to destroy
the convict labor lease system.
In 1891 they were called
        "Communists!"

In 1934 in a Kentucky jail death
        cell
with three men sentenced to die
I learned the song:
"Shut up in the Mines at Coal
        Creek"
from one on his way to the Chair.
Stanzas were found when 28
        bodies
were excavated
on a scrap of paper blood smeared
between lumps of coal.

Something of America I love
and cherish with warm pride
and something I intensely dislike:

Lundlow…!
Coal Creek!
Clifton and Mary Bryant!
John Woody and Effie!
Bill Blizzard!
Florence Reece!
Cabin Creek!
Bloody Harlan—corporate
        profits!
John D. Rockefeller the fourth:
"Too rich to steal."

Ludlow…!

                    Don West

(*In a Land of Plenty*, West End Press, 1982)

"So when the mines started. . . they organized
the union. I don't remember what year it was,
but we had the awfullest strike you ever saw.
There wasn't no big checks then. There wasn't
no handouts. We was on our own."
> The Reverend Tag King
> *We Be Here When the Morning Comes*

The Strike: A Bird's Eye View

I

It is the dead of winter.
The school bus is stuck up to its axle
in mud. The bus driver is cursing.

I sit with my sister on a leather seat.
It's split badly. The cotton padding
bursts through, and the springs cut
out bottoms.

Up ahead is the bridge, crooked
like an elbow. Each day the weight
of the bus makes it sink a little bit lower.

No one sits with us because our daddy
is picketing, and we wear underpants
made from flour sack cotton.

I dream of being a great fiddler
and making it to the Grand Ole Opry.

II

It's the first of March.
The icicles hanging from the eaves
have rainbows in them.

The kitchen is full
of the economics of coal dust
and sticking it out
for minimum wages.

Momma is cooking the last
of the fried ham and gravy.

She bends over the black wood stove
pumping heat into the room like
a weight lifter. Her belly bulges.

John L. Lewis, John L. Lewis:
Daddy repeats his name like
a powerful refrain in a song
about going to heaven.

The gourd hanging from the wall
glints like a penny.

Outside
the icicles come crashing down,
one after the other.

III

There's a sudden freeze in April.
My sister's gray dress
is torn at the waist.
My toes are blue and swollen.

Scabs slice up my daddy's face.
All over his cheeks, little red lips
pucker, pus at the corners.

A gun thug bombs
the front porch of our cabin.
Momma's belly sags
like a sack of potatoes.

For lunch at school now
we have only one biscuit to eat.
Nobody laughs
when we walk and our soles
flap on our feet.

In the mornings, I break the ice
around the pump and peer into
a world clear and fresh as a bell.

In the evenings Momma leaves us
and walks two miles
to visit our daddy in jail.

IV

It is May Day, and Momma,
in her new thin body,
is doing the washing.

The scrub board bubbles
with blue, her fists make knots
of our clothing.

I can smell our family ties
on their hooks, the coat
of white paint on the table,

my own untidy hair,
newly washed, and the breath
of my sister as she bends

prayerfully over the pages
of her geometry. Outside
a cardinal sings the first
two notes of "Annie Laurie."

For the second day in a row
we've had nothing to eat.

No one
has anything to say.

On the hillside
where MawMaw and PawPaw sleep
Daddy's digging
another much smaller grave.

V

Deep summer, smelling of roses:
I am cracking walnuts
and whistling through the gap
between my two front teeth.

The North Star trembles.
A pot of leather britches
boils on the stove.

We are all in the kitchen
with Daddy, who talks about
farming the coal. It's
a big black tree, secret

and deep inside the earth
falls the dark fruit
he brings home to us in white
flour, sugar, coffee, tobacco
hard candy.

He says
sometimes in the light
of the carbide lamps
veins flash
like the constellations of Orion.

The strike is over.
The gourd turns
the wind into music.

Llewellyn McKernan

(*Short and Simple Annals*, 1978)

Picket Line in Autumn

The face getting brown
as morning falls
just ripe out of the sky—
a change from last night's
cold, warm gloves and
frost poured into
these empty coffee cups—

you've never been so much
in the world as now,
spending all daylight
and all night too outdoors,
going in circles like the world does,
though sometimes it seems
standing still, getting nowhere—

except you know your tired feet
are turning the earth
and someday the sun
will give itself up to you,
the leaves surrender—
you know they will, if
you keep on walking long enough.

Mary Fell

(*The Persistence of Memory*, Random House, 1984)

The Last Unmined Vein

Now it's neither here nor there
to most folks
but then I've never figured myself
to be like many
much less most
I know what they do
no matter what they say
I know how they come
with trucks bigger than ary road
can hold
and drive her through yer yard
and right up on the porch
and park her next to yer rocking chair
and you ain't got a howdy-do
to say about it neither
once you put yer name
on that paper
that's it

Now my daddy and me
we used to dig a little coal
out of that vein across the bottom
Just a pick and a shovel
and what could be wheelbarrowed
out of there
was all that was took
and didn't hurt nothing
and kept a fire real good
and that's it
but that ain't what they got in mind
They wanting to make steel in Ohio
turn on the lights in New York City
and heat houses in Detroit

Shoot—I don't know a soul
in the whole state of Michigan
but that ain't really it
It ain't my business what they do with it
but this farm and everything that's in it
is plenty my concern
and I know how they come
with their mouths full of promises
and leaving with every one
of your fields full of ruts
and the mud sliding down the hillside
right onto your back steps
and there ain't a creek left
what would hold a living thing
and that's it
and the money
just don't mean that much to me
I done seen all I need to see
about where that money goes
and what's got with it
Last thing this country needs
is another new mobile home
with a four-wheel drive truck
parked on a mudbank in front of it
and that's it
and not another thing to show
for where and what your mammy and pappy
and their mammy and pappy
not to mention your own self and family
always had

So when that man in his new suit
and smooth as silk talking
came to my door
I didn't even ask him in
Said I wasn't interested

He laughed and said he wasn't selling
Said I didn't figure I was either
and that was it
Of course, I know he'll be back
but probably after I'm dead and gone
and if the children want to be so foolish
as to put an end
to what came long before them
ain't nothing I can do about it then
but I been laying plans
to remind them
to what it's gonna cost them
I done got my marker
and laid out the lines for my grave
right smack in the middle
of that vein
They gonna have to chip out the coal 6 foot by 6
and then put her right back on top of me
and that will be the end of that

Lee Howard

(*The Last Unmined Vein*, Anemone Press, 1980)

The Broad Form of the Company's Deeds

(Grandad all you bought was the air)

... and excepting and reserving all the coal
and other minerals
and other substances
on, in, and underlying said land
together with the right
of removing and taking away
the coal and other minerals
and other substances
from adjoining and adjacent land
through any openings
and the right to occupy
as may be necessary or convenient for mining purposes
without reservation or hindrance
and with proper rights for ventilation
and draining the mines
and all rights
of ingress, egress, or way
and the privilege of constructing
operating and maintaining railroads
and other roads
in, on, under, across, through and over the land
without being in any way liable
for any injury or damage which may be done to the land
or water therein upon
and generally free, clear and discharged
of and from all servitude to the land
                              whatsoever.

Bob Henry Baber

(A Picture from Life's Other Side, 1994)

Buzzsaws in the Rain, *or*
The Longer Between Fires, the Better

I know all the reasons
        for ending this knee-jerk
                assault on a steamroller,
        these mosquito drill drone,
        ping pong ball full of dead fish,
        stinking, rotting, rancid slop bucket
                full of pork barrel projects &
                senate chamber glories (or
                Bobby Byrd's thousand fiddles
                playing when that great gash
                slashes the Phelps Kentucky Pleasure Dome
                        in two)
                                blues

But none of them reasons
        make any sense so

        I just
                got to keep
                on thinkin about
                Rocky Pharoah & Arch Enema,
                Noah Flood & Nasty Bunion

        Ka-thunk, Ka-thunk
                past them
                to them

Broke lung, bent back, can't pay for the truck
        cause it's rollin over my leg, standin
        up to be counted and they hit me in the head,
        throw me in the garbage can & roll me over
        the hill into the river on Sunday my one day
        off till I start on the hoot owl
                                tonight too
                                        blues

Yeah, I know all the reasons
        but someday Rocky Pharoah
               when they ain't nothin
                    left to tear up
        and the lines are straight and true,

Stand in that white house, look at it all, all
        that you've done. Then may you
               ram your fist
        through the pane, slice up
        your arm, shit your blood, &
        fuck a buzzsaw in the rain

                Jim Webb

       (*Pine Mountain Sand and Gravel* {review}, 1984)

The Strikers

arisen from the smoke
and anxiety
of their paydays
and nights
they bribe their children
with peanuts and candy
to leave;
and leaning against the bar
they stare into mid-space
nodding in low talk;

and limping men
circle the table
grimly shooting nine-ball
with no bets down;

the storm blows open
the double doors,
cigarettes roll
still burning in sawdust;
and outside car horns blare
and men shout that it's time;
hands on hats
      they walk into rain

Joseph Barrett

(*Now & Then Magazine*, Spring 1988)

The Campfires of the Hunters

(The economics of controlled harvesting)

At night
the deer move out off the ridge to graze.
One of the older does
raises her graying head to gaze
with silently accepting eyes
far down the mountain at the blaze
of the campfires of the hunters.
Tomorrow they will kill her for food.

They will need the meat.
The winter will be long and cold
and the high cost of fuel for heat
will cut into the budget.

The doe does not own the land on which she is killed.
The hunters do not own the land on which they kill her.
The State owns the land.

The State regulates the hunters
and they've purchased licenses to avoid fines.
When they've finished their hunt,
they'll return to their homes,
and their jobs in the mines.
They mine coal from under the land.

They do not own the coal they mine.
The Coal Company does not own the coal they mine.
The Bank owns the coal.

The State sells the mineral rights
of the land to the Bank.
The Bank leases the mining rights
of the coal to the Coal Company.
The Coal Company mines the coal
and sells it to The Power Company.
The Power Company burns the coal
and produces fuel to run the mines
and to heat the homes of the miners.
The Bank owns a controlling interest
in The Power Company.

The fuel bills will be so high
because The Power Company
was granted a rate increase
by The State,
which sells the rights to The Bank,
which leases their interest to The Coal Company,
which sells the coal to The Power Company,
which is controlled by The Bank
and regulated by The State.
The Power Company sells power
to The State, to The Bank, to The Coal Company,
and to the miners.

At morning
the miners come yawning from the shaft,
dark, minstrel faces
with eyes
that have seen
the hunter's fires.

Kirk Judd

(Now and Then Magazine, Activism Issue, Fall 1990,
Tao-Billy, Trillium Press, 1996)

Speaking in Tongues

Crosses have appeared on Appalachian hillsides—
sudden testaments to a fire in the bones;
witness to a faith that has been translated
into crumbling tipples and railroad tracks,
into rusting automobiles and trestle bridges;
testimony to the conviction of miners
and of miners' wives, who seal their love
against the day when the Free Will Baptists
and the Old Regulars, the Hard Shells
and the snake-handlers
pray the corpses out of their coffins
to reclaim the land in the name of the redbud and the May apple,
for the dogwood, the sumac, and the ironweed.

Edwina Pendarvis

(*Human Landscapes*, with Philip St. Clair and Daniel
Smith, Bottom Dog Press, 1997)

The Strip Miner's Psalm to John C.C. Mayo
Holy Father of the Broad Form Deed

Lord John is my shepherd; I shall not want.
He maketh me to tear down hills and green pastures:
He leadeth me beside the stale waters.
He restoreth my soil with fescue; he leadeth me in
paths of D9's for his name's sake.
Yea, though I mine through the valley of the shadow of death,
I will fear no evil: for MSHA and OSHA art with me;
Thy rod and thy transit they comfort me.
Thou preparest a table before me in the presence
of my wife, her children, my children—and Aunt Berthie.
Thou anointest my head with blood, sweat and tears;
My cup runneth over with acids and sulfates.
Surely Demerol, Percocet and Workman's Comp shall follow me
all the days of my life:
And I will dwell in a doublewide forever.

G.C. Compton

I Am Looking

I am looking
for an Appalachian Ferlingetti
to shinny down
from his hip tree
and hew
with his broadax
just one
genuine log house
from the scraps
left on Pound Mountain's
strip mined ridges.

I am looking
for an Appalachian Ginsberg
to run howling
from St. Paul
through the fields
of Draper Valley
in search
of a mountain
till he gives up
at the Meadows of Dan
and sits cross-legged
on talus
while preaching
his own version
of the "Sermon on the Mount."

I am looking
for an Appalachian Kerouac
to come hitching
along The Trail of the Lonesome Pine

where he is plagued
by a convoy
of coal trucks
conjuring dust devils
during his search
for Nirvana
while bumblebees
on Queen Anne's lace
join his persistent OMMMMM.

I am looking
for Superman
to stop doing
whatever he is doing
with Lois Lane
just long enough
to fly
to eastern Kentucky
and restore gutted hills
to the way they were
when Daniel Boone
first walked over them.

I am looking
for Roy Rogers
to saddle up Trigger
and ride
out of his Victorville Museum
all the way
to what's left of Black Mountain
without encountering
one steep hill
so I can peep
at the bliss

he carries
in his saddlebags
while he sings
to me again,
"Happy Trails."

M. Ray Allen

The Pearl

Egyptian GEM wants to haul my heaven away
but the earth is the Lord's and his it's gonna stay
but, Lord, it just ain't right, so I pray with all my might
Lord, don't let 'em take my heaven away.

Them ol' corporapers wanna mess our happy home
we need to all get together tell 'em leave our heaven alone.
boys are you ready to fight? No words are gonna make it right
you can't discuss negotiatin' with the business end of a gun.

My mamma told me, "Child, West Virginia is your pearl
ain't no other place like it nowhere else in this world"
and Massey's gonna have a fight
if they think they can rob us blind
take away our mountains and steal our precious pearls.

I like Texas and I like Tennessee
but when you're talking West Virginia that's when
        you're talking to me.
Buddy, don't you put her down
there's more than coal in the ground
there's blood in the soil and that's where they'll bury me.

These Appalachian Mountains just as far as the eye can see
stretchin' out into the distance for miles they beckon me
I can hear em when I lay me down, Massey don't you
        come around
before you mess with my mountains
you're gonna have to mess with me.

Massey don't you put her down
there's more than coal in the ground
there's blood in the soil and that's where they'll bury me.

T. Paige Dalporto

(Solid Pearl, Mountain Whispers CD, 2006)

To Those That Refuse

The cellist of Sarajevo, Vedran Smailovic,
refused, insisted music transcend
the indiscriminate shelling
of the Innocents.

And in Tiananmen Square
the anonymous pedestrian
dared the tank
run over him.

Or in Knott County
the widow Combs
likewise dared
the stripmine dozer.

Or Rosa Parks
refusing to move
to the back of the bus
that Montgomery, Alabama day.

All saying *no* to the everyday
aggression of the Men and the Lie,
the business-as-usual
wrong-headedness of our worst ways.

In History these exemplars
to awaken the passive sleepwalkers
who live in days of terror, an acquiescence
to the nightmares of righteous wars

with the rationalism of knee-jerk patriotism,
no matter which nation rallies before which flag.

Jonathan Greene

(*Damn the Caesars* {review}, 2005)

Weaving Water

1.

Rafting the New River,
she wears the river's
pearl and crystal, raveling
and unraveling strands of water.

Perilous and imperiled,
the river shines
and crinkles ahead;
or stone-flurried, it foams, white
and unwearied in the narrows.

The rapids called "Surprise"
hidden behind the one-story boulder
tell and retell their tale
of white noise as she nears:

how water's violent but inviolate
force thumps, batters and lifts the raft
before it plummets prow-first
into the well of rock the water has worn
where the raft is caught, churns, surfs,
then escapes, shot out, to plow
through the next rift

in the rocks, where the onrushing
white water, a wave
in the momentum,
an apex in
the transparency, lifts
the raft, the snub bow
buoyed, rising—until sheer

force expels the boat, out,
down and up, on
to the river's quick glass,

where finally wide shallows weave
and unweave the almost sheer
tendrils of water under
the lettuce-green skin.

The raft is afloat now,
parting the pictures
of the gorge's pink walls,
the narrow river-shaped sky.

Below a trout flicks
its scales like Black Hills
gold, shining green, pink, yellow,
as it swims away
through the glaze.

For days, her hair gives off the smell
of river-silt, of mist and blue algae.

2.

That year, the spring rains in the Appalachians
loosened dogwoods' rust-spotted crosses of bloom.
The slippery grey branches shone like the practical
unbeautiful flumes of the steel mills
and the wet loaves of lumber stacked by the stone-
cast spindles of shadow downslope toward
the pit where coal was dug, where the dogwoods
dropped their white four-part flowers, luckless
clovers in the moonlight. The bituminous nights
fit snugly into the folds of the human-
sized hills. Come walk with me by the bone-pit,
she wrote you, near the run licked by chicory, ironweed
and white locust. See: one stray pear tree
blooms in the clear—refugee, pioneer.

Mary Moore

The Protests at Blair

Them assholes coming up here, outsiders trying to tell us we can't
strip mine. How would you like it if somebody tried to take
your farm away, or your steel mill or your line of business
selling computers? These are our mountains and we can do
with them what we want.

Massey buys the best equipment in the world—get on a dozer and you
can move anything—I mean, you want to get somewhere, just
auger a cliff, dynamite it, and in no time flat we'll have a road
the Governor could ride on, a road wide enough for the coal
trucks and the industry we need right here in West Virginia.
The Commissioner says so and I'm standing right behind him
with a dozer to back us up.

Our lives depend on coal and if you think I'm not going to rock those
protesters you're crazy. We'll heckle them off Blair Mountain
and clear out of Logan County. I'd do more than that, myself.
I'd be slashing tires and breaking out windows. It'd be buck-
shot I'd use. I'd pepper their flabby asses so they couldn't
set down for a month.

You should see what Dal-Tex's done up there on the mountain.
There's clover and blackberries and alfalfa—now, who ever
heard of alfalfa before in Logan County?—there's turkey and
deers and ducks everywhere—and hardwoods, too, they're
coming back.

I'd set up roadblocks and I got a deer rifle, too, and a bow, and I can
use the traps I bought for them black bears in the news. We
got the law on our side and we got God, too, ask Reverend
Bledsoe, he'll tell you, "and let them have dominion over all
the earth."

It's the Walker Machinery Company down there in Charleston
providing us with our equipment. You going to shut them
down? Or shut down Union Carbide and Dow? What about
the coal trucks out there on Highway 52? You going to stop
them? What about Allegheny Power? Or the coke for the
steel plants?

It really gripes my ass, them coming up here in their Jeep Cherokees
and Ford Explorers and Land Rovers—and in shorts, mind
you, and with brand-new workboots on, canvas vests and
ballcaps they just bought—stupid do-gooders trying to tell us
who were born here, who have homes here and work here,
what we can and can't do.

Dumb-asses. Don't they know stripping coal saves lives? When was
the last time you heard of a strip miner killed on the job, in a
slatefall or a gas explosion or getting black lung? What's worth
more, a man's life or a mountain? You ought to know the
answer. I sure as fuck do.

And that idiot journalist over there in Charleston—I read ever one of
his slanted articles, and each time I got mad all over again.
Somebody needs to take him down a notch or two, as in
catching him on the street and breaking his typewriter fingers,
along with his nose and a half-dozen teeth.

If any bastard environmentalist thinks they're going to tell me I can't
make a living at decent pay with what God provided us then
they'd better look over their shoulder, the tree-hugging bitches
and faggots. The god-damned communists. I'd blow them
back to hell where they come from.

Victor Depta

(*Azrael on the Mountain*, Blair Mountain Press, 2002)

Sundial

The biggest coal slurry pond ever built
hangs on the mountain above my school.
Massey says the dam is safe, but in Kentucky
black water poured through a Massey dam
and killed a river. On rainy days
I sit in Marsh Fork School and listen
for the roar of water. On sunny days
I grab my desk when the bombs
that blast the mountaintops rattle the school.
On blasting days two girls in my room
hide under their desks, sitting in the black
from the coal dust that sifts in through the windows
and the cracks in the walls. Our famous silo,
where coal falls into the trains, casts shadows
on the school and dumps dust into the air.
People keep saying there's nothing we can do.
A newsman came and showed the world
the Marsh Fork Elementary School coal silo.
He showed the plant where poisons wash the coal
and fill the valley with bad air that makes us sick.
When I ask about the leaking dam and the coal dust
and the poison air, my daddy says coal keeps me fed.
He warns me, "Never join the mountain huggers
with their marchin' and sittin' and trespassin'."
He says Massey will fire him and we'll starve to death.
I'm thinking he's wrong.
I'm thinking if I get to grow up and be a man,
I will fix the bad things in the Coal River Valley.
That is, unless the coal runs out and Massey moves on
to turn another river valley upside down.
I'm thinking I will stand in their way.

                    S. L. Gardner

AFTERWORD

By Jack Spadaro

Maggie Anderson writes in the poem "Long Story," which can be found in this anthology, "In West Virginia a good story takes awhile / And if it has people in it, you have to swear / That it is true." The poems in this collection are true—all of them. They come to us from the deep hollows and coal towns and rivers and the front porches and pool halls and coal mines in authentic and lyrical voices that will not go away.

I began my work in the coalfields of southern West Virginia on Buffalo Creek, Logan County, in the spring and summer of 1972. I had been sent there to investigate the causes of a coal-waste dam failure and flood that had taken the lives of a hundred-and-twenty-five men, women, and children and wiped out seventeen communities. I remained in the coalfields of West Virginia, eastern Kentucky, and southwestern Virginia for the next thirty-four years, doing what I could to alleviate the environmental and health and safety hazards caused by coal mining. I stayed so that I could continue hearing the voices—the same voices we find in this fine gathering of poetry from a region and people who are very much alive and fighting for their lives every day.

The faces and the voices I remember from Buffalo Creek still haunt me. The poems in this collection have the same effect—from P.J. Laska's homage to a forgotten coal town in the New River Gorge to Billy Edd Wheeler's "They Can't Put It Back." All of the poems kept coming back to me with their clear images of a people who continue, regardless of the difficulties and tragedies, to keep growing and struggling and triumphing, like (as Dick Hague writes) "new brier, tough over blackened land."

I have made my life in these hills among these brave and dignified people, and I will never leave them. Their poetry is in their eyes, in their language and songs, and in their everyday lives. The poems in this volume have told their story in a lasting way. The gentlest poet among them, James Still, in his first book of poems *Hounds On The Mountain* (1937), wrote in the poem "Heritage":

> I shall not leave these prisoning hills
> Though they topple their barren heads to level
> earth
> And the forests slide uprooted out of the sky
> . . . .
> Being of these hills I cannot pass beyond.

And so it is for me and for many of the poets who have contributed to this anthology. Blair Mountain Press and the editors, Chris Green and Edwina Pendarvis, have made a beautiful work.

Jack Spadaro

Books, Films, and Web Sites about Coal & Central Appalachia

The bibliography is organized under the topics listed below:

About Coal (by State Governments)

Accidents & Safety

African-American Miners

Black Lung

Buffalo Creek

Coal Industry

Coal Towns

Community & Power

History & Culture

Language

Labor Struggles: Harlan County, Kentucky

Labor Struggles: UMWA & Mother Jones

Labor Struggles: West Virginia

Literature

Song

Stripmining and Mountaintop Removal

Women

About Coal (by State Governments)

Kentucky. *Kentucky Coal Education*. Kentucky Office of Energy Policy. Division of Fossil Fuels & Utility Services.
http://www.coaleducation.org/

Kentucky. *Coal*. Kentucky Geological Survey. University of Kentucky. http://www.uky.edu/KGS/coal/coal_information.htm

Ohio. *Coal Mining*. Mineral Resource Management. Ohio Department of Natural Resources.
http://www.dnr.ohio.gov/mineral/coal/index.html

Virginia. *Coal in Virginia*. Virginia Division of Mineral Resources. Department of Mines, Minerals, and Energy.
http://www.dmme.virginia.gov/Dmr/DOCS/MinRes/COAL/coal.html

West Virginia. Division of Mining and Reclamation. West Virginia. Department of Environmental Protection. http://www.wvdep.org/item.cfm?ssid=9

Accidents & Safety

Braithwaite, John. *To Punish or Persuade: Enforcement of Coal Mine Safety.* Albany: State University of New York Press, 1985.

Hume, Brit. *Death and the Mines: Rebellion and Murder in the United Mine Workers.* New York: Grossman, 1971.

Humphrey, H. B. *Historical Summary of Coal-Mine Explosions in the United States, 1810 [i.e 1910]-1958.* Washington: U.S. Govt. Print. Off., 1960.

Mine Safety and Health Administration. United States. Department of Labor. www.msha.gov.

Mining Safety and Health Research. "Coal Mining Disasters (Incidents with 5 or more fatalities)." United States. National Institute for Occupational Safety and Health. http://www.cdc.gov/niosh/mining/statistics/discoal.htm

Mining Safety and Health Research. United States. National Institute for Occupational Safety and Health. http://www.cdc.gov/niosh/mining

Office of Miners' Health Safety &Training. West Virginia. Department of Commerce. http://www.wvminesafety.org/

Richmond, JK et al. U.S. Department of the Interior, Bureau of Mines, Information Circular 8909, "Historical Summary of Coal Mine Explosions in the United States, 1959-81." http://www.cdc.gov/niosh/mining/pubs/pubreference/ic8909.htm

African-American Miners

Lewis, Ronald L. *Black Coal Miners in America: Race, Class, and Community Conflict, 1780-1980.* Lexington: University Press of Kentucky, 1987.

Trotter, Joe William. *Coal, Class, and Color: Blacks in Southern West Virginia, 1915-32.* Urbana: University of Illinois Press, 1990.

Black Lung

Derickson, Alan. *Black Lung: Anatomy of a Public Health Disaster.* Ithaca: Cornell University Press, 1998.

Smith, Barbara E. *Digging Our Own Graves: Coal Miners and the Struggle over Black Lung Disease.* Philadelphia: Temple University Press, 1987.

Whetstone, Stephanie Wagner. *Fighting for a Breath.* Documentary. Whitesburg, KY: Appalshop, 1995.

Buffalo Creek

Bethell, Thomas N. and Davitt J. McAteer. *The Pittston Mentality: Manslaughter on Buffalo Creek.* Huntington, WV: Appalachian Movement Press, 1972

Erikson, Kai. *Everything in its path: destruction of community in the Buffalo Creek flood.*
New York: Simon and Schuster, 1976.

Nugent, Tom. *Death at Buffalo Creek: The 1972 West Virginia Flood Disaster.* New York: Norton, 1973.

Pickering, Mimi. *The Buffalo Creek Flood an Act of Man.* Documentary. Whitesburg, KY: Appalshop, 1975.

- - -. *Buffalo Creek revisited.* Documentary. Whitesburg, KY: Appalshop, 1984.

Stern, Gerald M. *The Buffalo Creek Disaster: The Story of the Survivors' Unprecedented Lawsuit.* New York: Random House, 1976.

Coal Industry

Caudill, Harry M. *Theirs Be the Power: The Moguls of Eastern Kentucky.* Urbana: University of Illinois Press, 1983.

Christenson, Carroll Lawrence. *Economic Redevelopment in Bituminous Coal: The Special Case of Technological Advance in United States Coal Mines, 1930-1960.* Cambridge, Harvard University Press, 1962.

Division of Fossil Fuels and Utility Services. Kentucky Office of Energy Policy. http://www.energy.ky.gov/dffus/

274

Goode, James B. *The Cutting Edge: Mining in the 21st Century*. Ashland, KY: Jesse Stuart Foundation, 2002.

Goodell, Jeff. *Big coal: The Dirty Secret Behind America's Energy Future*. Boston: Houghton Mifflin Co., 2006.

Hamilton, Walton Hale and Helen R. Wright. *A Way of Order for Bituminous Coal*, New York, Macmillan Co., 1928.

Hansell, Tom. *Coal Bucket Outlaw*. Documentary. Whitesburg, KY: Appalshop Film & Video, 2002. Depicts the lives of coal truck drivers.

Lockard, Duane. *Coal: A Memoir and Critique*. Charlottesville: University Press of Virginia, 1998.

Long, Priscilla. *Where the Sun Never Shines: A History of America's Bloody Coal Industry*.
New York: Paragon House, 1989.

Seltzer, Curtis. *Fire in the Hole: Miners and Managers in the American Coal Industry*. Lexington: University Press of Kentucky, 1985.

West Virginia Coal Association. http://www.wvcoal.com/

Coal Towns

Shiftlett, Crandall A. *Coal Towns: Life, Work, and Culture in Company Towns of Southern Appalachia, 1880-1960*. Knoxville: University of Tennessee Press, 1991.

Eller, Ronald. *Miners, Millhands, and Mountaineers: Industrialization of the Appalachian South, 1880-1930*. Knoxville: University of Tennessee Press, 1982.

Peterson, Bill. *Coaltown Revisited: An Appalachian Notebook*. Chicago: Regnery 1972
Francaviglia, Richard V. *Hard Places: Reading the Landscape of America's Historic Mining Districts*. Iowa City: University of Iowa Press, 1991

Gillenwater, Mack Henry. *Cultural and Historical Geography of Mining Settlements in the Pocahontas Coal Field of Southern West Virginia, 1880 to 1930*. Knoxville, TN: University of Tennessee, 1973.

History & Culture

Crowell, Douglas L. *History of the Coal-Mining Industry in Ohio*. Columbus: Ohio Dept. of Natural Resources, Division of Geological Survey, 1995.

Gaventa, John. *Power and powerlessness: Quiescence and Rebellion in an Appalachian Valley*. Urbana: University of Illinois Press, 1980.

Hennen, John C. *The Americanization of West Virginia: Creating a Modern Industrial State, 1916-1925*. Lexington: University Press of Kentucky, 1996.

Fones-Wolf, Ken and Ronald L. Lewis. *Transnational West Virginia: Ethnic Communities and Economic Change, 1840-1940*. Morgantown: West Virginia University Press, 2002.

Morris, Homer Lawrence. *The Plight of the Bituminous Coal Miner*. Philadelphia: University of Pennsylvania Press, 1934

Tams, W. P. *The Smokeless Coal Fields of West Virginia: A Brief History*. Morgantown, West Virginia University Library, 1963

Lewis, Ronald. *Transforming the Appalachian Countryside: Railroads, Deforestation, and Social Change in West Virginia, 1880-1920*. Chapel Hill: University of North Carolina Press, 1998.

Labor Struggles: Harlan County, Kentucky (and region)

Ewen, Lynda Ann. *Which Side Are You On? The Brookside Mine Strike in Harlan County, Kentucky, 1973-74*. Chicago: Vanguard, 1979

Garland, Jim and Julie S. Ardery. *Welcome the Traveler Home: Jim Garland's Story of the Kentucky Mountains*. Lexington: University Press of Kentucky, 1983.

Hevener, John. *Which Side Are You On? The Harlan County Coal Miners, 1931-1939*. Urbana: University of Illinois Press, 1978.

Jones, G. C. *Growing Up Hard in Harlan County*. Lexington: University Press of Kentucky, 1985.

Johnson, Anne Lewis. *Justice in the Coalfields*. Documentary. Whitesburg, KY: Appalshop, 1995. United Mine Workers strike against the Pittston Coal Company.

Kopple, Barbara. *Harlan County U.S.A.* Documentary. Burbank, CA: RCA/Columbia Pictures Home Video, 1976.

National Committee for the Defense of Political Prisoners and Theodore Dreiser, ed. and. *Harlan Miners Speak: Report on Terrorism in the Kentucky Coal Fields*. [Harcourt, Brace and Co., 1932.] New York, Da Capo Press, 1970.

Scott, Shaunna L. *Two Sides to Everything: The Cultural Construction of Class Consciousness in Harlan County, Kentucky*. Albany: State University of New York Press, 1995.

Labor Struggles: UMWA & Mother Jones

Aurand, Harold W. *From the Molly Maguires to the United Mine Workers: The Social Ecology of an Industrial Union, 1869-1897*. Philadelphia: Temple University Press, 1971.

Clark, Paul F. *The Miners' Fight for Democracy: Arnold Miller and The Reform of the United Mine Workers*. Ithaca: New York State School of Industrial and Labor Relations, Cornell University, 1981.

Fox, Maier Bryan. *United We Stand: The United Mine Workers of America, 1890-1990*. [Washington, D.C.]: United Mine Workers of America, 1990.

Gorn, Elliott J., *Mother Jones: The Most Dangerous Woman in America*. New York: Hill and Wang, 2001.

Johnson, Anne Lewis and Buck Maggard. Documentary. *Roving Pickets, 1961-1965*. Whitesburg, KY: Appalshop, 1991.

Jones, Mother, *Autobiography of Mother Jones*. [Chicago, C.H. Kerr & Co., 1925.] New York: Arno, 1969.

Laslett, J. H. M., ed. *The United Mine Workers of America: A Model of Industrial Solidarity?* University Park: Pennsylvania State University Press, 1996.

Mine War on Blackberry Creek. Documentary. Whitesburg, KY: Appalshop, 1986. Overview of the ongoing strike of union coal miners against the A.T. Massey Co. and includes an intimate look at both workers and strike breakers and chronicles the UMWA's

Mulcahy, Richard P. *A Social Contract for the Coal Fields: The Rise and Fall of the United Mine Workers of America Welfare and Retirement Fund*. Knoxville: The University of Tennessee Press, 2001.

Perry, Charles R. *Collective Bargaining and the Decline of the United Mine Workers*. Philadelphia: Industrial Research Unit, the Wharton School, University of Pennsylvania, 1984.

Labor Struggles: West Virginia

Corbin, David. *Life, Work, and Rebellion in the Appalachian Coal Fields: The Southern West Virginia Miners, 1880-1922*. Urbana: University of Illinois Press, 1981.

Corbin, David, ed. *The West Virginia mine wars: an anthology*. Charleston, WV: Appalachian Editions: Distributed to the trade by Trans Allegheny Books, 1991

Fagge, Roger. *Power, Culture, and Conflict in the Coalfields: West Virginia and South Wales, 1900-1922*. Manchester: Manchester University Press, 1996

Lane, Winthrop D. *Civil War in West Virginia*. [New York, B.W. Huebsch, Inc., 1921.] New York: Arno, 1969.

Lee, Howard Burton. *Bloodletting in Appalachia: The Story of West Virginia's Four Major Mine Wars and Other Thrilling Incidents of its Coal Fields*. Morgantown: West Virginia University, 1969.

Lunt, Richard D. *Law and Order vs. the Mines: West Virginia, 1907-1933*. [Hamden, Conn.: Archon Books, 1979.] Charleston, WV: Appalachian Editions/Trans-Allegheny Books, 1992.

Sayles, John and Chris Cooper. *Matewan*. Movie. Irvine, CA.: Lorimar Home Video Inc., 1987.

Savage, Lon. *Thunder in the Mountains: The West Virginia Mine War, 1920-21*. Pittsburgh, Pa.: University of Pittsburgh Press, 1990.

Shogan, Robert. *The Battle of Blair Mountain: The Story of America's Largest Labor Uprising*. Boulder, CO: Westview Press, 2004.

Sullivan, Ken, ed. *The Goldenseal book of the West Virginia Mine Wars: Articles Reprinted from Goldenseal Magazine, 1977-1991*. Charleston: Pictorial Histories Pub. Co., 1991.

Language

Preston, Dennis Richard. *Bituminous Coal Mining Vocabulary of the Eastern United States.* American Dialect Society, no. 59. Tuscaloosa, AL: University of Alabama Press, 1973.

Puckett, Anita. *Seldom Ask, Never Tell: Labor and Discourse in Appalachia.* New York: Oxford University Press, 2000.

Literature (Novels, Poetry, Criticism)

Angle, Barbara. *Rinker.* Washington: Crossroads Press, 1979.

- - -. *Those that mattered.* New York: Crown Publishers, 1994.

Danford, Harry Edmund. *The West Virginian.* New York: H. Vinal, 1926.

Depta, Victor. *Azrael on the Mountain.* Ashland, KY: Blair Mountain Press, 2002. (Poems on Mountaintop Removal)

Duke, David C. *Writers and Miners: Activism and Imagery in America.* Lexington: University Press of Kentucky, 2002.

Giardina, Denise. *Storming Heaven.* New York: Norton, 1987.

- - -. *The Unquiet Earth.* New York: Norton, 1992

Goode, James B. *Poets of Darkness.* Jackson: University Press of Mississippi, 1981

- - -. *Up From the Mines.* Ashland, KY: Jesse Stuart Foundation, 1993.

Hankla, Cathryn, *A blue moon in Poorwater.* New York: Ticknor & Fields, 1988

Hauser, Lisa Kay and Dale Smith. *Turn Back Time.* Tacoma, WA: Golden Anchor Press, 2000.

House, Silas. *Clay's Quilt.* Chapel Hill, N.C.: Algonquin Books of Chapel Hill, 2001.

- - -. *The Coal Tattoo.* Chapel Hill, NC: Algonquin Books of Chapel Hill, 2004.

Mooney, Stephen Douglas. "'Coal dust in our blood': Central Appalachian coal mining culture in the American novel." Dissertation. University of Kentucky, 1998.

Settle, Mary Lee. *Choices*. New York: Nan A. Talese/Doubleday, 1995.

- - -*The Killing Ground*. New York: Farrar, Straus, Giroux, 1982.

- - - . *The Scapegoat*. New York: Random House, 1980.

Smith, Lee. *Fair and Tender Ladies*. New York: Putnam, 1988.

- - -. *Oral History*. New York: Putnam, 1983

Still, James. *On Troublesome Creek*. New York: Viking Press, 1941.

- - - . *River of Earth*. New York: The Viking Press, 1940.

Yount, John. *Hardcastle*. New York: R. Marek Publishers, 1980.

Stripmining and Mountaintop Removal

Johnson, Anne Lewis. *On Our Own Land*. Documentary. Whitesburg, KY: Appalshop Films, 1988. Citizens rise against the Broad Form Deed.

Caudill, Harry M. *My Land is Dying*. New York: E.P. Dutton, 1971.

Lewis, Anne and Buck Maggard. *To Save the Land and People*. Documentary. Whitesburg, KY: Appalshop, 1999.

Kentuckians for the Commonwealth. (Citizens' Action Group). "Canary Project." http://www.kftc.org/our-work/canary-project

Ohio Valley Environmental Coalition. Citizen's Action Group. http://www.ohvec.org/

Montrie, Chad. *To Save the Land and People: A History of Opposition to Surface Coal Mining in Appalachia*. Chapel Hill: University of North Carolina Press, 2003.

Johannsen, Kristin, Bobbie Ann Mason, and Mary Ann Taylor-Hall, eds. *Missing Mountains: We Went to the Mountaintop but It Wasn't There*. Nicholasville, KY: Wind Publications, 2005.

Reece, Erik. *Lost Mountain: A Year in the Vanishing Wilderness: Radical Strip Mining and the Devastation of Appalachia*. New York: Riverhead Books, 2006.

McSpirit, Stephanie. *Martin County Project: Researching Issues & Building Civic Capacity After an Environmental Disaster*. Eastern Kentucky University and the Appalachian Regional Commission.

http://www.anthropology.eku.edu/MCSPIRIT/Martin_Cnty_Final_Report.htm

Committee on Coal Waste Impoundments. National Research Council. *Coal Waste Impoundments: Risks, Responses, and Alternatives.* Washington, D.C.: National Academy Press, 2002.

"Mining the Mountains." *Charleston Gazette.* A comprehensive site listing all stories the Gazette has published on MTR from 1998 through the current day.
http://www.wvgazette.com/section/Series/Mining+the+Mountains

Office of Surface Mining. United States. Department of the Interior. http://www.osmre.gov/

Office of Surface Mining Reclamation and Enforcement. United States. Deptartment of the Interior. *Report on October 2000 breakthrough at the Big Branch Slurry impoundment Martin County Coal Corporation, Big Branch Slurry impoundment, Martin County, Kentucky.* [Washington, D.C.]: Office of Surface Mining, 2002. http://purl.access.gpo.gov/GPO/LPS20094

Office of Surface Mining. *2/23/99 Mountaintop Mining Report to Congress* http://www.osmre.gov/mt022399.htm (for list of reports see: http://www.osmre.gov/mtindex.htm)

Vietor, Richard H. K., *Environmental Politics and the Coal Coalition.* College Station: Texas A & M University Press, 1980.

Song

Carawan, Guy and Candie Carawan. *Voices from the Mountains.* New York: Knopf, 1975.

Green, Archie. *Only a Miner: Studies in Recorded Coal-Mining Songs.* Urbana, University of Illinois Press, 1972.

Korson, George Gershon. *Coal Dust on the Fiddle: Songs and Stories of the Bituminous Industry.* Philadelphia, University of Pennsylvania Press, 1943.

Romalis, Shelly. *Pistol Packin' Mama: Aunt Molly Jackson and the Politics of Folksong.* Urbana: University of Illinois Press, 1999.

Women

Barret, Elizabeth. *Coalmining Women*. Documentary. Whitesburg, KY: Appalshop, 1982.

Giesen, Carol A. B. *Coal Miners' Wives: Portraits of Endurance.* Lexington: University Press of Kentucky, 1995.

Moore, Marat. *Women in the Mines: Stories of Life and Work.* New York: Twayne Publishers, 1996.

Norris, Randall and Jean-Philippe Cypres. *Women of Coal.* Lexington: University Press of Kentucky, 1996.

Roberts, Ronald and Carol Cooke-Roberts. *Mother Jones and Her Sisters: A Century of Women Activists in the American Coal Fields.* Dubuque, IA: Kendall/Hunt Publishing, 1998.

Anthologies

There have been five other key anthologies that either focused on or included poems about culture and mining in Appalachia. Below we list poems in the four that also appear in *Coal*. The fifth anthology focuses on twelve poets writing about the anthracite fields in Pennsylvania: *Coalseam: Poems from the Anthracite Region*. Karen Blomain, ed. Scranton, PA: University of Scranton P, 1996.

Mucked. **Jim Webb and Bob Henry Baber, eds. Williamson, WV: Hesperus P, 1977. Reprinted with the Southern Appalachian Writers Cooperative in 1984.**

Gail Amburgey, "Blood Money"
Bob Henry Baber, "Cold Knob, Relcaimed"
Baber and Jim Webb, "Almost Heaven, Almost Hell"
Joseph Barrrett, "The Strikers"
Michael Henson, "Poem for Jim Trammel"
P.J. Laska, "Song of Terry"
Jim Wayne Miller, "The Brier's Pictorial History of the
       Mountains"
Bob Snyder, "Spring in Glen Jen"

Old Wounds New Words: Poems from the Appalachian Poetry Project. **Bob Henry Baber, George Ella Lyon, and Gurney Norman, eds. Ashland, KY: Jesse Stuart Foundation, 1994.**

Gail Amburgey, "3 A.M. Train" and "Blood Money"
Carley Rees Bogarad, "My Father's Black Lungs"
James B. Goode, "Poets of Darkness"
Lee Howard, "The Last Unmined Vein"
Jim Webb, "The Day the X-Man Came"

Wild Sweet Notes: Fifty Years of West Virginia Poetry, 1950-1999. **Barbara Smith and Kirk Judd, eds. Huntington, WV: Publishers Place, 2000.**

Maggie Anderson, "Long Story"
Mary Joan Coleman, "Noah Totten"
Lloyd Davis, "Farmington No. 9"
Kirk Judd, "The Campfires of the Hungers"
Margaret McDowell, "The Child's Song" and "Traveling
       Song"
Bonni McKeown, "Coal Miners Off Duty"

Irene McKinney, "Deep Mining" and "Twilight in West Virginia: Six O'Clock Mine Report"
Edwina Pendarvis, "Augury"
Don West, "There'll Be a Tomorrow"
Billy Edd Wheeler, "Christmas in Coal Town"

Working Classics: Poems on Industrial Life. **Peter Oresick and Nicholas Coles, eds. Urbana, IL: University of Illinois P, 1990.**

Harley Elliot, "Numbers"
Mary Fell, "Picket Line in Autumn"
June Jordan, "From America: A Poem in Progress"
Suzanne Matson, "Love in the Coal Mines"
Ed Ochester, "Retired Miners"
James Wright, "Honey"
Robert Wrigley, "Miners Shaking Hands with a Union Man"

284

Permissions

Unless noted below, permission to print or reprint poems in this anthology was granted by the authors who hold the copyrights. Every effort has been made to obtain publication rights from both living poets and families of deceased poets. In a few cases no literary heirs of deceased poets were located. We invite artists or their heirs to contact us.

"Long Story," "Mining Camp Residents, West Virginia, 1935," and "Spitting in the Leaves" are from *Windfall: New and Selected Poems,* by Maggie Anderson, © 2000. Reprinted with permission of the University of Pittsburgh Press.

"My Father's Black Lungs" by Carley Rees Bogarad; © Estate of Carley Rees Bogarad. Reprinted with permission of Len Bogarad.

"Go Tell the Children" by Muriel Miller Dressler; © William Plumley. Reprinted with permission of William Plumley.

"The Last Unmined Vein" by Lee Howard; © Estate of Lee Howard. Reprinted with permission of Tamarra De Ridder.

Excerpt from "From America: A Poem in Progress" by June Jordan; © June Jordan. Reprinted by permission of the June M. Jordan Literary Estate Trust, www.junejordan.com

"Thomas Mason Kelly In a Moment of Unrest" by John F. Keener; © *Appalachian Journal,* permission to reprint granted by John F. Keener and *Appalachian Journal.*

"Best House They Were Ever In," "Coal Fern," "Monongah," and "Company" are from *Hill Daughter: New and Selected Poems,* by Louise McNeill and Maggie Anderson, © 1991. Reprinted with the permission of the University of Pittsburgh Press.

Copyright by the Estate of Jim Wayne Miller; the poems "Abandoned," "Shapes," and "The Brier's Pictorial History of the Mountains," by Jim Wayne Miller, are reprinted from his book *The Brier Poems* (1997) with permission of Gnomon Press.

"Spring in Glen Jean" by Bob Synder; © Estate of Bob Snyder. Reprinted with Permission of Margaret Snyder.

Author Index

Contributors

Jenny Persinger Adams is an English teacher at Montcalm High School in Mercer County, West Virginia. She is a 2006 graduate of Marshall University, where she received her MA in English. She earned her undergraduate degree in Secondary English Education from Concord University in 2004. While at Concord, Jenny worked for the student literary magazine, *Reflexes*. Her poem "The Beaches of Normandy" appeared in its spring 2004 issue. She enjoys writing poetry that embraces her Appalachian culture, particularly her family's experiences in and around West Virginia's coal mines.

Christine Orchanian Adler is a writer and editor whose poetry has appeared online at *The Furnace Review* and *LiteraryMama.com*. She earned her master's degree in creative writing from Manhattanville College and is editorial consultant to the literary journal *Inkwell*. Her articles and book reviews have appeared in various publications throughout the Northeast region. She lives in New York with her husband and two sons.

M. Ray Allen has three books of poems: *The Roads I Travel* (1990), *Between the Thorns: Windcarver Songs of Appalachia* (1991), and *Beyond Star Bottom and Other Poems* (2000). Allen (born in1941 in Martin, KY) is the son of Ralph E. Allen, a coal miner from Floyd County, Kentucky, and Pauline Hall Allen, a school teacher from the same county. He completed his BA and MA at Morehead State University (MSU), and made his debut as a poet in 1968 as a featured reader at the Douglass House Center in Long Beach, California. He received his MFA in writing for television and motion pictures from UCLA in 1980. Currently, Allen, a retired teacher, owns and operates The Buckhorne Country Store and Campground in Clifton Forge, Virginia, where he serves as director of The Alleghany Highlands Poetry Workshop for the Clifton Forge Library and Appalfolks of America Association (AAA), a non-profit corporation he founded in 1985. In 1991 he was inducted as the 81st member of the MSU Alumni Hall of Fame.

Gail V. Amburgey, born and raised on Buffalo Creek, in West Virginia, was one of the founders of Soupbean Poets of Antioch/Appalachia. Her poems have appeared in *What's a Nice Hillbilly Like You . . .; We're Okay but We Ain't Special; Mucked; New Ground*; and *Old Wounds, New Words*. Amburgey currently makes her home in Frankfort, Kentucky.

Maggie Anderson is the author of four books of poems, most recently *Windfall: New and Selected Poems* (2000). Anderson is also the editor of *Hill Daughter, New and Selected Poems of Louise McNeill* and co-editor of *Learning by Heart: Contemporary American Poetry about School*, and *A Gathering of Poets*. Currently she is the director and a member of the faculty in the Northeast Ohio MFA program at Kent State University, where she directs the Wick Poetry Center and edits the Wick Poetry Series of the Kent State University Press.

Mark Anderson, born in Roane County, WV, graduated from Bard College where he was awarded the Wilton Moore Lockwood Prize for his poems, *Workings*. He holds an MA degree in Speech and Communications from West Virginia University. He teaches at Ravenswood High School, Jackson County, WV, where he has received numerous awards for his contributions to public education, including Jackson County Teacher of the Year and Language Arts Teacher of the Year. "Searching for Ideas in Things," a motivational writing assignment and video publication, won the RESA V Teaching Technique Award. His work appears in such publications as *Croton Review, Katuah Journal, Now & Then Magazine, Limestone, Riverwind, Laurel Review, Connecticut River Review, Dialogue, Nomad's Choir*, and *Gambit*.

Bob Henry Baber is the current mayor of Richwood, WV. He is the inventor of the "lowku" poetry form, performs original children's stories, and conducts creative writing workshops throughout the Appalachian region.

Marietta Ball lives in Xenia, Ohio, where she writes poetry and fiction. Her recent poetry placements are with the *Journal of Kentucky Studies* and *Now & Then Magazine*. Her short stories have appeared in *M Magazine*, the *Dayton Daily News*, and *MOTA 3: Courage* (Triple Tree Press).

Joseph Barrett (1950-1990) was born in Montgomery, WV, and went to high school in Richwood, at the southern end of the Monongahela National Forest. He attended Bethany College and studied at Oxford and in the Middle East. He is internationally published, his poems appearing in literary journals in Japan, France, and Australia, as well as the U.S. In 1988, he co-edited *Venue*, a literary anthology. He published two poetry collections, *Roots Deep in Sand* and *Periods of Lucidity*, and had completed a third, *Blue Planet Memoirs*, at the time of his death.

Elaine Bentley Baughn was born in Jenkins, Kentucky, the fifth child of seven. Her father worked in the mines in his youth and drove a coal truck until strip mining resulted in less and less work for him. Eventually he had to take his family out of the mountains to survive. Baughn's work has appeared in the journal *Gone, Volumes 1* and *II; Through Spider's Eyes;* and the *Ballard Street Poetry Journal.* Forthcoming poetry will appear in *Moon Journal* (Fall/Winter 2006). She is the author of four collections, the latest of which, *Portraits and Landscapes,* is due out in late 2006. She credits her Appalachian heritage for her work ethic and her passion for recycling.

Laura Treacy Bentley is a writer from Huntington, West Virginia, whose work has been published in the United States and Ireland, in *The New York Quarterly, Art Times, Rosebud, Poetry Ireland, Crannog,* and *The Stinging Fly,* among others. Her poetry was featured on *A Prairie Home Companion* website and *Poetry Daily.* One of her poems, "The Quiet Zone: Green Bank Observatory," appears on posters available for purchase at the observatory's Galaxy Giftshop: (*www.gb.nrao.edu*)

Roy Bentley is the author of nine books of poems, including his most recent collection, *The Trouble with a Short Horse in Montana,* which won the 11th Annual White Pine Press Poetry Prize in 2005 and is scheduled to be published this fall by White Pine Press. In 2001, he was awarded a National Endowment for the Arts individual artist fellowship in poetry and has won Ohio Arts Council individual artist fellowship in poetry six times. Bentley (whose roots are in eastern Kentucky, Letcher County) lives in Stuart, Florida, where he recently completed a novel about a man who hears what he takes to be the voice of God command: *Go, start me a dive team.* The novel is called *Arc of the Diver.*

Carley Rees Bogarad (1935-1995) was born and educated in West Virginia, and chaired the English Department at the State University of New York, New Paltz, from 1985 to 1995. She authored the textbook *Legacies: Fiction, Poetry, Drama, and Non-Fiction* (Wadsworth, 1995), which has now gone into its third edition, and her book of poems is called *Outrageous Fortune* (St. Andrews College Press, 1995).

Jeanne Bryner was born in Waynesburg, Pennsylvania, and lived in West Virginia until age four. A graduate of Trumbull Memorial Hospital School of Nursing and Kent State University's Honors College, Bryner has won awards for nursing and community service as well as for writing. Her first collection of poems, *Breathless,* was published in 1995 as part of the Wick Series by Kent State University Press. Her collection *Blind Horse* was published by Bottom Dog Press in 1999.

Joseph Caldwell is an attorney in Charleston, West Virginia. His chapbook, *Sabbatical on Winifrede Hollow,* was published in 1993 by Trillium Press (St. Albans, West Virginia), with a second edition appearing in 1998. In 1992 he won a writer's fellowship from the West Virginia Commission on the Arts. Caldwell's poems also appear in Barbara Smith and Kirk Judd (eds.), *Wild Sweet Notes: Fifty Years of West Virginia Poetry 1950-*

1999 (Publishers Place, 2000). Caldwell received his BA degree from West Virginia University in 1969, his law degree from the University of Florida in 1974, and was admitted to the West Virginia bar in 1974. He was born in 1947 at Charleston, West Virginia. "Buffalo Creek" was first published in *Hindman Settlement School Anthology*.

Wanda D. Campbell is a writer, artist, and teacher from southern Kentucky's western-most Appalachian county, a unique pocket of America known as Upper Cumberland, "the land where the Mountains meet the South." Campbell writes predominantly about southeastern Kentucky and its culture, the region she knows best. Her work has been included in journals such as *Taproot Literary Review, Mid-South Review, Story South, Pegasus, River Walk Journal, Other Voices International* and many other publications, both traditional and online.

Sheila L. Carter-Jones earned her PhD in English education from the University of Pittsburgh. She is an active member of the National Council for the Teachers of English and a teacher consultant for the Western Pennsylvania Writers Project at the University of Pittsburgh. She is one of the few but growing number of Nationally Board Certified teachers in the Pittsburgh Public School District, where she has been teaching for over thirty years. Dr. Carter-Jones has also taught various courses in the education department of several local colleges and universities. The courses included teaching *The Teaching of Writing* to young people entering the teaching profession. Also included in her repertoire are numerous writing workshops which she has developed to help motivate and act as scaffolds for novice and young writers. Carter-Jones credits the domestic working women in the small coal mining community where she grew up as the spiritual source of her poetic inspiration. Much of her personal writing highlights the people and events in that small community of hard-working people. Her poetry is published in several anthologies and journals including *Crossing Limits, Pittsburgh Quarterly, Pennsylvania Review, Tri-State Anthology*, and *Riverspeak*.

Grace Cavalieri has written fourteen books and chapbooks of poetry; her latest children's book is *Little Line*. Her collection of poetry *What I Would Do For Love*, poems in the voice of Mary Wollstonecraft (1759-1797) (Jacaranda Press, 2004), won a 2005 Paterson Prize. The play from this story, *Hyena in Petticoats*, had its first staged reading in 2006 at the New York Public Library. Her play *Quilting the Sun* was recently presented at the Smithsonian Institution by its New York cast and will receive a world premiere in 2007 at Centre Stage, South Carolina. Her 20th play, *Jennie & the JuJu Man*, premiered in NYC, 2004. She produced and hosted *The Poet and the Poem* on public radio for 29 years. The series is now recorded at the Library of Congress for distribution via NPR. Grace has won the Allen Ginsberg Award for poetry, the PEN-Fiction Award for short story, and the Silver Medal from the Corporation for Public Broadcasting. She won the 2005 Bordighera Award, which will publish her book *Water on the Sun* in Italian and English, Fall 2006.

James E. Cherry is a poet, fiction writer, educator, and social critic.

Mary Joan Coleman considers her writing enriched by her Appalachian heritage. She says of her writing that she "writes of lived experience and the struggle to retain dignity and courage through the tragedies and comedies that distort our lives. . . . Mine is blood art; I slash at the arteries of social, personal, and ethnic consciousness—not as a violent political convert, but as liberator of those elements vital to the spirit of endurance. I write what I have lived; growing up on the backroads of America, alone and broke on the urban streets, plagued by fear and alienation, back home in the coal rush era sifting through the remnants of my past. I write of personal struggles that can have universal affinity. I speak of crushing disappointments and startling triumphs, in my own life and in the lives of others. . . . My poems are affirmations of life and truth." (From *Take One Blood Red Rose*, West End Press, 1978)

G.C. (Gayle) Compton was born November 3, 1944, at Big Shoal, an early Pike County, Kentucky, coal camp. He was educated at Pikeville College and Morehead State University. He has worked as a coal miner, mail carrier, English teacher and broadcast journalist. His prose and poetry have appeared in *The Kentucky Poetry Review, Wind, Appalachian Heritage, Ideals, Saw* (UK), *The Kentucky Anthology,* and elsewhere. He has earned numerous writing awards including the *Appalachian Heritage-*Plattner Award for Writing Excellence, the *Kudzu Magazine* Poetry Prize for 2005, and the Kentucky Newspaper Award for Best One-Subject Column. He is preparing for publication a book-length collection of his short stories entitled *Black Lung Washing Machine: The Peabrook Kentucky Stories.* Compton lives at Jonancy, in Pike County, with his wife and nine cats.

Sarah L. Cornett-Hagen is a native of Haymond, Letcher County, Kentucky. She currently lives quietly in southern Oregon at Still Point with her husband, Warren, two cats, and one African hen. Still Point is her touchstone for nature essays, poetry and philosophical writings. She credits her writing group, "Hay Wire," for keeping her focused and on track. Her most recent publications have appeared in *Poetry as Prayer: Appalachian Women Speak* (2004), *More Kisses* (Feb. 2005), *Go Haywire: An Anthology of Ashland Writers* (2005), and *The Rag* (#95).

Caitlin Cunningham graduated from Marshall University in 2006 with a BA in Psychology and will begin her MA in Social Work at West Virginia University in the fall, 2006. She plans on working with children and families in rural West Virginia.

T. Paige Dalporto has won awards for his poetry, photography, and his songwriting. His recording of "The Pearl," which he wrote for Coal River Mountain Watch, was included on MountainWhispers.com Audio Books compilation CD, *When Miners March*, along with two of his other songs. Dalporto's poetry has been published in *Wild Sweet Notes II; Appalachian Heritage Magazine; Appalachian Journal; Open Minds Quarterly;* and in the online publications *Litvision, Niendergasse,* and *Muse Apprentice Guild*. His photography has appeared in the WV Juried Exhibition, Tamarack, The Museum in the Community, and at The Wheeling Artisan Center. In July 2006, he completed an album of original songs, *Solid Pearl*. Website www.tpaige.com.

Lloyd Davis, a native of West Virginia, is the grandson of two certified mine foremen. In 1996 he retired as Professor Emeritus from West Virginia University where he taught Humor in American Literature and Creative Writing. From 1966 to 1968 he was the editor of *Appalachian Review*, published by the University's Appalachian Center. His poems have appeared in *The Ohio Review, The Georgia Review, Kansas Quarterly, Foxfire, Three Rivers Poetry Journal, Southern Poetry Review,* and many other periodicals. In 1982 he won the Annex 21 national poetry prize with *The Way All Rivers Run* which was published by the University of Nebraska at Omaha Press. Other collections include *Fishing the Lower Jackson* and *Stars in the Dark*. His poems have been included in several anthologies, including *This Book Is a Movie* (Delta Books, 1971) and *Art Work, No Commercial Value* (Grossman, 1972).

Mary Lucille DeBerry worked many years in Morgantown for West Virginia Public Television, where she produced historical, cultural, and public affairs series, segments, and programs. Her poems have appeared in *Appalachian Heritage, Appalachian Journal, Grab-a Nickel, Now & Then Magazine, Traditions,* and the anthology *Wild Sweet Notes*.

Mark DeFoe is Professor and chair of the English department at West Virginia Wesleyan College. His six published chapbooks include *The Green Chair* (Pringle Tree Press, 2003) and *Mark DeFoe's Greatest Hits* (Pudding House, 2004). His latest book is *The Rock and the Pebble*. DeFoe has conducted workshops for writers of all ages and has read his work at colleges, libraries, and art centers. His work has been published in numerous anthologies and has appeared in Internet e-zines and journals across the country, including *Poetry, Yale Review, Paris Review, Kenyon Review,* and *Sewanee Review*. A former Bread Loaf Scholar, DeFoe has been recognized by awards from *Appalachian Heritage, The Atlanta Review, Tulane Review, Black Warrior Review, Smartish Pace, Nimrod, Chautauqua Literary Review,* and *Now & Then Magazine*. He has received two Artist Fellowships from the state of West Virginia (1998 and 2003). DeFoe lives in Buckhannon, West Virginia, with his wife, a pianist and music teacher.

Cheryl Denise and her husband, Mike Miller, are a part of the Shepherds Field intentional community near Philippi, West Virginia. She is the author of the poetry book, *I Saw God Dancing*, co-published by Cascadia Publishing House and Herald Press.

Victor M. Depta is the publisher of Blair Mountain Press. He has also authored eight books of poetry, a trilogy of novels, two volumes of plays and a collection of essays.

Muriel Miller Dressler (1918-2000) was born and lived in the Kanawha Valley, West Virginia. Although she never completed high school, she learned her love of words (including Shakespeare and Chaucer) as she helped her mother plant their garden. She published both *Appalachia, My Land* and *Appalachia* in 1973 with Morris Harvey College (now University of Charleston). Dressler was a vital and dynamic presence, and she read her work throughout the region and beyond until the mid-1980s when she suffered a heart attack and necessarily withdrew from public performance.

Harley Elliot is a writer and visual artist in Salina, Kansas. He is the author of children's books and nine collections of poetry, including *Animals that Stand in Dreams* and *Darkness at Each Elbow* (both available from Hanging Loose Press, Brooklyn, New York), as well as *The Monkey of Mulberry Pass* (1991, Woodley Press, Topeka, Kansas). His first nonfiction book, *Loading the Stone*, is forthcoming from Woodley Press.

Mary Fell was raised in a working-class neighborhood in Worcester, Massachusetts. She attended local schools, worked as a social worker, and eventually found her way to poetry. Her poems about work have been reprinted in many anthologies, and were first collected in her book, *The Persistence of Memory* (Random House, 1984). She lives and teaches in Richmond, Indiana.

Diane Gilliam Fisher was born and raised in Columbus, Ohio. Her parents were part of the Appalachian outmigration—her father from Johnson County, Kentucky, her mother from Mingo County, West Virginia. Fisher has a PhD in Romance Languages and Literatures from Ohio State University and an MFA from the Warren Wilson Program for Writers. In 2003 she received an Ohio Arts Council Individual Artist Fellowship. Her books include *Recipe for Blackberry Cake*, in the Wick Poetry Chapbook Series from Kent State University Press (1999); *One of Everything* (2003), from the Cleveland State University Poetry Center, and *Kettle Bottom* (Perugia Press, 2004), a collection of poems written in the voices of people living in the coal camps at the time of the West Virginia mine wars. Smith College chose *Kettle Bottom* as the common reader for its incoming class, 2005. Fisher won the Ohioana Library Association

Book of the Year Award in Poetry 2005 for *Kettle Bottom*, which also won a Pushcart Prize and was an American Booksellers Association Book Sense Pick for the Top Ten Poetry Books of 2005. She teaches at Converse College in Spartanburg, South Carolina.

Jason Frye received his BA from Marshall University in 2000 and MFA in Poetry from the University of North Carolina, Wilmington, in 2005. His poetry has appeared in *Ellipsis,* and his interview with the late Robert Creeley appears in *Crazyhorse.* Frye lives in Wilmington, North Carolina, with his wife, and works as a woodwright while he is compiling his first collection of poetry. He is originally from Logan, West Virginia; his family still lives there.

Jenny Galloway is a poet, playwright, and song writer from Letcher County, Kentucky. She has authored two books of poems, *Blackberry Tea* (1988) and *A Cave and A Cracker* (1996), and two plays, *Stonega Run* and *Sycamore House.* She has also produced a CD called *Stonega Run* with Doc Frazier and the Clyde Stanly Band. Her work has been published in *Mountain Review, Appalachian Heritage, Mountain Life and Work, Now & Then Magazine, Pine Mountain Sand and Gravel,* and *New River Free Press, Back Home in Kentucky, Hill and Valley, Heartland Review, M Magazine,* and *Truckers USA.* Anthologies in which she has appeared include *Step Around the Mountain, Harvest from the Hills, The Best of Hill and Valley,* and most lately in *Writing Who We Are: Poems by Kentucky Feminists* (1999) and *Poetry as Prayer: Appalachian Women Speak* (2004). Galloway is now gratefully living back on the home place where she was raised.

Sharon Gardner grew up in Bedford, Pennsylvania. She taught school for five years and has worked in academic, school, and public libraries. While she and husband Joe lived in "The Bluefields," West Virginia coal mining captured her attention, and she became a "student of coal." After the Gardners moved to Fairmont, West Virginia, in 1996, Sharon wrote coal camp features for the Fairmont *Times West Virginian.* In 1997 Bob Armstead contacted her, and they decided to collaborate on a book about his life. The University of Tennessee Press published *Black Days, Black Dust: The Memories of an African American Coal Miner* [as told to S. L. Gardner] in 2002. She is currently working on her first novel, which is "coal related—and unique." Because she was inspired by a poem from her young adult poetry manuscript, "Mirrors" (first place winner on the Wall of Poetry at WV Writers' Conference in 2006), Sharon wrote "Sundial," her first published poem.

Harry Gieg grew up in North Philadelphia, in Pennsylvania, but has lived and worked in Huntington, West Virginia, for the past 27 years. Although the themes, images, rhythms, and diction of his poetry most often reflect this earlier urban experience, his poems reflect his Appalachian experience as well. His early involvement with vocal and percussive music (late-forties, early-fifties R&B group singing, Afro-Cuban music, and jazz) have been influences on especially the lyric aspects of his writing. He's published in *Appalachian Journal, Jacaranda, Earlham Review, Pennsylvania Review*, and other journals—and in the anthologies *Tobacco*, by the Kentucky Writers' Coalition; *Guyandotte Poets*, by Trillium Press; and *Wild Sweet Notes II*, by Publishers Place. He's a recipient of an NEA-funded West Virginia Commission for the Arts Fellowship Award for poetry. He and poet Eddy Pendarvis co-authored the chapbook *Duets*, by Shoestring Press.

James B. Goode, creative writer, essayist, photographer, and Appalachian scholar, has written about the Appalachian region since undergraduate school in the 1960's. His major published works include *Applachian Mountain Mother* (1969), *The Whistle and the Wind* (1971), *Poets of Darkness* (1981), *Up from the Mines* (1993), *Ancient Sunshine: The Story of Coal* (1997), and *The Cutting Edge: Mining in the 21st Century* (2002). His documentary films include *Lynch: A Coal Legacy* and *Coal, Steel, Machines, & Men: The Benham Story* which were recently broadcast on Kentucky Educational Television. James lives in an 82-year-old house on a farm in Anderson County, Kentucky, with his life partner Donna Slone, where they write, farm blackberries and blueberries, and hold summer camp for six beautiful grandchildren.

Jonathan Greene is author of twenty-five books, most recently *Fault Lines*; *On the Banks of Monks Pond: The Thomas Merton / Jonathan Greene Correspondence* (both Broadstone Books 2004); and *The Death of a Kentucky Coffee-Tree* (Longhouse, 2006). Forthcoming: *Gists, Orts, Shards: A Commonplace Book* (Broadstone Books) and *Hut Poems* (Mountains and Rivers Press). He lives on the Kentucky River with his wife, the weaver and photographer Dobrée Adams.

Richard Hague is author of twelve books, including *Milltown Natural: Essays and Stories from a Life in Ohio* and *Alive in Hard Country*, winner of the 2004 Appalachian Writers Association's Poetry Book of the Year. He was born and raised in Steubenville, Ohio, across the river from Weirton, West Virginia. He teaches in Boston and Cincinnati. Hague is a member of the Southern Appalachian Writers Cooperative and edited the SAWC journal, *Pine Mountain Sand & Gravel*, for a number of years.

James Harms has published four books of poetry, the most recent of which are *Freeways and Aqueducts* (2004) and *Quarters* (2001) from Carnegie Mellon University Press; a fifth collection, *After West*, will appear in 2008. Newer work is in recent issues of *The Gettysburg Review, Oxford American, Ploughshares, Verse, The North American Review, Shenandoah, Crazyhorse*, and others. He directs the MFA Program in Creative Writing at West Virginia University and was awarded a NEA Fellowship in 2005.

Brooke Haynes grew up in the weeds and water of Harlan County as a coal miner's daughter. In 2005, she graduated with a BA in English from Transylvania University and has had poetry published by Transy's art and literary journal, *The Transylvanian*. Currently she is knee-deep in the world of non-profit development and is the Special Events Coordinator at Hospice Care Plus, Inc. in Berea, Kentucky. She now lives in Lexington with a basset hound named Buford.

Kenneth D. Haynes comes from a legacy of coal miners in Harlan, Kentucky, where he now works as a land surveyor and is an active member of the Grays Knob Bible Church. His poetry has appeared in *Appalachian Heritage*, and he continues to pull from his experiences growing up in the mountains of eastern Kentucky to enrich his writing.

Michael Henson is author of the novel *Ransack* and the short-story collection *A Small Room with Trouble on My Mind*, both with the West End Press. His chapbook of poems, *The Tao of Longing*, was published in 2005 by Dos Madres Press. *Crow Call*, an extended elegy for his friend Buddy Gray, an activist with the homeless who was murdered by a former client, is due out in fall 2006 from the West End Press. Henson lives in Cincinnati, where he works with the urban Appalachian community. He is a member of the Southern Appalachian Writers Cooperative.

Jane Hicks, a native of East Tennessee, is an award-winning poet and quilter. She won the 2000 Appalachian Poetry Contest sponsored by *Now & Then Magazine*. She also won the James Still Award for Poetry given by the Appalachian Writers Association. The Jesse Stuart Foundation published her first book, *Blood and Bone Remember: Poems from Appalachia* in 2005. The book met with popular and critical acclaim, winning the Appalachian Writers Association Poetry Book of the Year prize. It was also nominated for the Appalachian Studies Association's Weatherford Award. Hicks' poetry has frequently appeared in journals and literary magazines in the southeast, notably *Wind, Now & Then Magazine, Appalachian Journal, Appalachian Heritage*; she also has work forthcoming in *Shenandoah*. Her poems have been anthologized in *Migrants and Stowaways; Literary Lunch*, published by the Knoxville Writers Guild; and *Crossing Troublesome: 25 years of the Appalachian Writers Workshop*. Her "literary quilts" illustrate the works of playwright Jo Carson and novelists Sharyn McCrumb and Silas House. The art quilts have toured with these respective authors and are the subject of an upcoming feature in a noted quilting magazine. Hicks teaches intellectually gifted students in Sullivan County, Tennessee.

Pamela Steed Hill is an editor for University Publications at Ohio State and a freelance writer for online literature reference publishers. She has had poems published in over a hundred journals, including *Antioch Review, Chicago Review, Nimrod, Potpourri,* and *South Carolina Review.* Three of her poems have been nominated for a Pushcart Prize. Her first collection of poems, *In Praise of Motels,* was published in 1999 by Blair Mountain Press.

Ron Houchin was born in 1947 in National City, California, and was raised in Huntington, West Virginia. For thirty years he taught composition, literature, and creative writing at Fairland High School, in Proctorville, Ohio. He's read all over the world, including at Bewleys International Café, Dublin; The Dublin Writers' Centre; Galway Arts Centre, Galway, Ireland; The Hemingway Days Writers' Conference, Key West; The Ypsilan Theater, Prague, Czech Republic; The James Wright Poetry Festival, Martins Ferry, Ohio; and the Southern Appalachian Writers' Cooperative, Highlander Center, New Market, TN. His latest book, *Among Wordless Things* (2005), was awarded Appalachian-Book-of-the-Year in poetry (2005) by the Appalachian Writers' Association (AWA).

Lee Howard (1952-2003), a native of Clay County, Kentucky, was the daughter of a hellfire preacher and a mother who wrote to her every day: Lee Howard was a voice for her place and her people. She held a BA from Morehead State University and two MAs, one in sociology (George Washington University) and one in comparative religion (Marylhurst College). Her work appeared in magazines such as *Southern Exposure, Mother Jones,* and *The Washington Review;* in anthologies, including *A Gathering at the Forks, Old Wounds, New Words,* and *Crossing the Troublesome;* and in her groundbreaking collection, *The Last Unmined Vein* (1980). She died too young but her words go on speaking.

Charlie Hughes, though employed as an analytical chemist, has an abiding interest in the literary arts. He runs Wind Publications (http://windpub.com) which specializes in Kentucky and regional writers and published *Missing Mountains* (2004). His poems and fiction have appeared in prominent literary magazines, including *Hollins Critic, Cumberland Poetry Review, Exquisite Corpse, Appalachian Heritage, Cincinnati Poetry Review,* and others. Hughes is editor of *The Kentucky Literary Newsletter,* a biweekly e-mail newsletter (http://windpub.com/current.. htm), and is author of *Shifting for Myself* (2002), a volume of poems.

Harry Humes was born and grew up in the small coal-mining town of Girardville, Pennsylvania. His recent poetry collections are *Butterfly Effect* (Milkweed Press, 1989), selected by Pattiann Rogers for the National Poetry Series 1998, and *August Evening with Trumpet* (University of Arkansas Press, 2004). He is the recipient of a National Endowment for the Arts Poetry Grant and several writing grants from the Pennsylvania Council on the Arts. His poem "Butterfly Effect" was chosen by James

Tate for B*est American Poetry of 1997*. He lives in the country, close to Kutztown, Pennsylvania, with his wife and daughter.

June Jordan (1936-2002) was born in Harlem. Poet, activist, teacher, and essayist, she was a passionate and inspirational voice for liberation. June Jordan lived and wrote on the frontlines of American poetry, political vision, and moral witness.

Kirk Judd, the Creative Writing instructor and Director of Allegheny Echoes Writing Programs, is from Huntington, West Virginia. He has taught workshops and presented material across the State in many venues for the WV Division of Culture and History, the WV Humanities Council, and other arts organizations. Kirk was co-editor of the highly praised anthology *Wild Sweet Notes: Fifty Years of West Virginia Poetry 1950 – 1999* (2000). A founding member and former president of West Virginia Writers, Inc., he has appeared at most of the State's regular fairs, concerts, and festivals. The author of two collections of poetry, *Field Of Vision* and *Tao-Billy*, he is internationally known for his performance work combining poetry and old-time music. In September of 1996, Judd's work was included in a South American cultural exchange and was translated and performed on university campuses and in native villages in Brazil. In 2001, he participated with other West Virginia artists, musicians, and singers in a series of performances of Appalachian-heritage arts in Ireland and Scotland.

Sandi Keaton-Wilson, of Somerset, KY, is a writer of poetry, prose, and plays. Her work has appeared widely in the Appalachian region, including *Poetry as Prayer: Appalachian Women Speak, Telling Stories: Fiction by Kentucky Feminists*, and *The Unveiling*, her first produced play by ACT (Actors' Collaborative Theatre, Pikeville, KY) in 2005. She enjoys traveling to do dramatic readings of her work.

John F. Keener was born and raised in Charleston, West Virginia. He earned his BA and MA degrees at the University of North Carolina at Chapel Hill and his doctorate at the University of Kentucky, all in English literature. He and his wife Stephanie, a native of Leslie County, Kentucky, moved to Banner Elk, North Carolina, in 1997, where John went to work for Lees-McRae College. He has served Lees-McRae as a member of the English faculty and in various administrative positions since then, currently filling the post of Dean of Planning, Research and Records. Aside from a variety of academic publications, he has published over a dozen poems in various periodicals, nearly all of which deal with the Appalachian region. There is coal mining in his family.

Debra J. Harmes Kurth resides in Milton, West Virginia, though she was raised in Wisconsin. She is the owner/editor of an emerging poetry quarterly, *Art with Words*; writes a weekly column on poetry for two local newspapers; is president of her local poetry society; and serves as 1st Vice President of the West Virginia Poetry Society. She is an award-winning poet on state and national levels and is published in *Lucidity, Black Widows Web of Poetry, Red River Review, Descending Darkness, Laurels, The WV Poetry Society Anthology,* and in *Beyond Katrina,* published by the Arts & Healthcare Initiative of Louisiana—a book of poems, quotes, and images inspired by Hurricanes Katrina and Rita. Debra is the primary editor of the chapbook *A place of . . . Amazing Grace,* which was put together as a tribute to West Virginia's miners and their families.

Walter Lane has been published on topics ranging from dynamiting fish to snake handling. He is fortunate to have all 9 and 7/8's fingers and a slight limp. Due to the alleged autobiographical nature of his work, regional magazines have labeled him eccentric. "Autobiography of a Nobody," his first published work, was published under fiction, to his chagrin. Others have sent him copies of his publications on occasion because he omitted data necessary for the publishing editor to locate him, which he found amusing. He has a checkered career of a range of jobs that includes coal mining. He is a social commentator who lives down the street from the Raccoon, Kentucky, post office.

P. J. Laska has authored eight volumes of poetry, writes essays, and is currently working on *Turning Words: New and Selected Poems.* Laska was raised in Farmington, West Virginia, which had five working mines within a mile or two of town where his family (father, sisters, and aunts) worked. Laska got his PhD in philosophy, focusing on Kant, and returned to WV to teach and write poetry and essays that grapple with politics, reality, and philosophy (most currently of the Taoist variety). He is now retired and writing in Beckley, West Virginia.

Christina Lovin lives in Lancaster, Kentucky, and teaches college writing classes in and around Lexington. Her writing has appeared in *Harvard Summer Review, Entelechy International, The Mid-America Poetry Review, New Southerner, Hunger Mountain, Missing Mountains: We Went to the Mountaintop but It Wasn't There,* and other periodicals and anthologies. Her poetry manuscript *What We Burned for Warmth* was selected as a semi-finalist for the Backwaters Press 2006 Poetry Prize. A chapbook of the same title was finalist for the Portlandia Press Chapbook Award. "Coal Country," a crown sonnet, was selected winner of the *Passager* Poetry Prize, 2005 Betty Gabehart Poetry Prize winner by Women Writers of Kentucky, and a finalist for the 2006 Rita Dove Poetry Award. She has studied in Harvard University's writing program, and holds an MFA in Creative Writing from New England College. She was a residency fellow at the Vermont Studio Center in the spring of 2006, where she began work on a large-scale poetry project involving the Ulster-Scots heritage and how it relates to Southern Appalachia. Lovin has been a recipient of two artists' grants from the Kentucky Arts Council.

Jeff Mann grew up in Covington, Virginia, and Hinton, West Virginia. He has degrees in English and forestry from West Virginia University. His poetry, fiction, and essays have appeared in many publications, including *Wild Sweet Notes: Fifty Years of West Virginia Poetry 1950-1999, Prairie Schooner, Shenandoah, Laurel Review, The Gay and Lesbian Review Worldwide, Crab Orchard Review, West Branch,* and *Appalachian Heritage.* He has published three award-winning poetry chapbooks, *Bliss, Mountain Fireflies,* and *Flint Shards from Sussex;* two full-length books of poetry, *Bones Washed with Wine* and *On the Tongue;* a collection of personal essays, *Edge;* a novella, *Devoured,* included in *Masters of Midnight: Erotic Tales of the Vampire;* a book of poetry and memoir, *Loving Mountains, Loving Men;* and a volume of short fiction, *A History of Barbed Wire.* He teaches creative writing at Virginia Tech in Blacksburg, Virginia.

Sandra Marshburn has poems appearing in various journals and anthologies. Her third chapbook, *Winter Beach,* was published in 2003 by Pudding House Publications. She teaches writing courses at West Virginia State University and lives in Charleston on the Elk River.

Suzanne Matson, born in Portland, Oregon, was educated in Oregon and Washington, and since 1988 has taught in the English department at Boston College. A recipient of a Massachusetts Cultural Council Fiction Writer's Fellowship, she has recently written the novel *The Tree-Sitter* (W. W. Norton, 2006). Her previous two novels, also from Norton and reissued in paperback by Ballantine, are *A Trick of Nature* (2000) and *The Hunger Moon* (1997). Her books of poems are *Durable Goods* (1993) and *Sea Level* (1990), published by Alice James Books. Many poems in these volumes were previously published in journals including *The American Poetry Review, Poetry, The Boston Review, Poetry Northwest, The Southern Poetry Review, Harvard Review, Indiana Review,* and *Shenandoah.* Her autobiographical, literary, and op-ed essays have appeared in periodicals such as *The New York Times Magazine, Child, The Seattle Times, The American Poetry Review, Harvard Review,* and *Mid-American Review.* She lives in Newton, Massachusetts, with her husband and three sons.

Margaret McDowell, from Morgantown, WV, has published two collections of poetry, *Our Song, Too,* and *View from College Avenue.*

Bonni McKeown, born in Philadelphia, PA, spent most of her life in Hampshire County, WV, and graduated from WVU School of Journalism in 1971. During five years in Beckley, WV, in the late 1970s, she worked as a reporter on the Beckley *Post-Herald* and then as a local staffer for Rep. Ken Hechler. She authored the biography, *Peaceful Patriot: The Story of Tom Bennett* (Mountain State Press, 1980) about a WVU student

302

conscientious objector who served as an Army medic in Vietnam. She also led a citizens' group, "Retain the Train," in a successful effort to keep the Amtrak "Cardinal" running through southern West Virginia, 1979-83, and an unsuccessful effort to stop the construction of the Corridor H four-lane highway through the wild mountains of eastern West Virginia. A blues piano player and singer-songwriter, she founded the Charleston WV Blues Society in 2006. Her writing appears in *Wild Sweet Notes* and in *The West Virginia Encyclopedia*.

Llewellyn McKernan has lived in and around Huntington, West Virginia, longer than anywhere else on earth. Here she has written and published three poetry books (*Short and Simple Annals, Many Waters,* and *Llewellyn McKernan's Greatest Hits*) and four children's books (*More Songs of Gladness, Bird Alphabet, This Is The Day,* and *This Is The Night*). She has an MFA in writing from Brown University and has taught English at Marshall University. Her poetry has appeared in *The Kenyon Review, Southern Poetry Review, Antietam Review, Kestrel, Poet & Critic, Now & Then Magazine,* and *Appalachian Journal*.

Irene McKinney was born and raised in Belington, West Virginia. She received her BA from West Virginia Wesleyan College, MA from West Virginia University, and PhD from the University of Utah. She has taught at Western Washington University; the University of California, Santa Cruz; and West Virginia Wesleyan, from 1991 until her retirement in 2000. She lives on a 35-acre portion of the family farm where she lived as a child. Her books of poetry include *The Girl with the Stone in her Lap* (1976), *The Wasps at the Blue Hexagons* (1984), *Quick Fire, Slow Fire* (1988), and *Six O'Clock Mine Report* (1989). She edited *Backcountry*, an anthology of contemporary West Virginia poetry and prose (WV University Press, 2002). Her most recent poetry collection is *Vivid Companion* (2004). Irene has been Poet Laureate of West Virginia since 1994.

Louise McNeill (1911-1993) was Poet Laureate of West Virginia from 1979 until her death. Her poetry collections are *Mountain White* (Kaleidoscope Press, 1931); *Time is our House,* (Middlebury College Press, 1942); *Gauley Mountain,* (Harcourt Brace, 1960); *Paradox Hill: From Appalachia to Lunar Shore,* (WV University Libraries, 1972); and *Elderberry Flood: The History, Lore, and Land of West Virginia Written in Verse Form,* (Elderberry Books, 1979). Maggie Anderson selected poems from these collections as well as previously unpublished poems for the anthology *Hill Daughter, New and Selected Poems by Louise McNeill,* (University of Pittsburgh Press, 1991).

Rob Merritt is a professor of English and a writer at Bluefield College, in Virginia, and has published poetry and nonfiction in a variety of journals, including *The Sow's Ear Poetry Review, Asheville Poetry Review, Confluence, The Potomac Review, Village Rambler.* His work also appears in the anthology *Wild Sweet Notes II: Contemporary West Virginia Writers*. Much of his writing concerns geography and the meaning of space. Living on the Virginia-West Virginia border, he says, "I see how people deal with the legacy of coal mining. I notice the pervasive beauty and pervasive environmental degradation. Somehow nature endures." Rob is an active member of West Virginia Writers, Inc.

Jim Wayne Miller (1936-1996), a native of the mountain country of North Carolina, was a mentor and promoter of Appalachian literature throughout his life. He graduated from Berea College and received his PhD in German and American Literature from Vanderbilt University in 1965. While at Vanderbilt, he studied under the Agrarian poet Donald Davidson and Hawthorne scholar Randall Stew. Miller was a Professor of German language and literature at Western Kentucky University for 33 years. He served as a consultant to the Appalachian Studies programs in Kentucky, Tennessee, and Ohio and was a visiting Professor in Appalachian Studies at the Berea College Appalachian Center. Miller worked in the Poet-in-the-Schools program in Virginia and directed poetry workshops for several universities. His books include *Copperhead Cane* (1964), *Dialogue with A Dead Man* (1974), *The Mountains Have Come Closer* (1980), *Vein Of Words* (1984), *Nostalgia for 70* (1986), *Brier: His Book* (1988), and *Newfound* (1989).

Mary Moore is a native Californian. A poet of places, she finds she has "written myself into" the West Virginia landscape during the 11 years she has lived here. She came in 1995 to teach poetry and Renaissance literature at Marshall University. Her first year of teaching at Marshall taught her a lot: "I had been told that 'you can't teach' books like Joseph Conrad's *Heart of Darkness* 'here,' but when I introduced this problematic and beautiful book, I asked the class what the role of ivory in *Heart* reminded them of in their own lives. 'Coal,' they said. It gave me the same kind of chill that Emily Dickinson said poetry gives. Coal is certainly at the heart of much darkness here." As a poet, Moore has published poems most recently in *Prairie Schooner, Sow's Ear Review, Literary Mama,* and *West Virginia Wild and Wonderful, V. II,* and earlier in *Poetry, Field, New Letters, Nimrod,* and others. Her collection of poems *The Book of Snow* (Cleveland State University Press, 1998) also bears traces, like West Virginia's landscape, of coal mining.

Phyllis Wilson Moore grew up in coal country, in Waynesburg, Pennsylvania, the rural county seat of Greene County, just a few miles above the Mason Dixon Line. She moved to West Virginia's coal country to attend Fairmont General Hospital School of Nursing in 1953. She married Jim Moore, a native West Virginian, in 1956. Since then the Moores have lived in Fairmont, Elkins, and Charleston. In 1987, Moore set about to research West Virginia's then little-known literary heritage. This personal hobby mushroomed and attracted the interest and support of scholars, historians, and teachers. Her efforts are now the nucleus of the first official literary map of the Mountain State and the foundation for two websites, *MountainLit*, hosted by the Bridgeport Library (<<u>www.mountainlit.com</u> >), and an electronic literary map of West Virginia, hosted by Fairmont State University. A writer as well as a reader, she devotes equal time to writing poetry, fiction, and nonfiction, researching the state's literature and literary sites, and promoting the state's extensive literary heritage.

Brenda Morris was the first woman at her mine. Eventually there were ten, including her two older sisters. She had the reputation among her workmates of being a skilled and hard worker. Her 4'11" height made it difficult to do some of the tasks of her job as a roofbolter, which involves drilling holes in the rock over a tunnel and then laminating the rock strata together with four foot bolts. Roofbolting is the most dangerous and one of the most strenuous jobs in the mines. Morris was laid off from the mines before dying of a heart attack several years ago.

Ed Ochester published most recently *The Land of Cockaigne* (Story Line Press, 2001). Forthcoming are his collections, *Unreconstructed: Poems Selected and New* (Autumn House, 2007) and *The Living Poem* (University of Pittsburgh Press, 2007), the latter an anthology of contemporary American poetry. He edits the Pitt Poetry series and is general editor of the Drue Heinz Literature Prize for short fiction (both from the University of Pittsburgh Press). He co-edits the poetry magazine *5 AM* and is a core faculty member of the Bennington College MFA program.

Delilah Ferne O'Haynes, EdD, is Associate Professor at Concord University in Athens, WV, where she teaches Creative Writing. O'Haynes is a coal miner's daughter from southwest Virginia. Her first book, *The Cacter of Mountains*, a collection of poetry and photography, is scheduled for release in 2006. Her second book, entitled *Walk Free from Fear of Cancer*, will be available shortly thereafter. She has published educational and literary articles and has also published both fiction and poetry for journals such as *The Sow's Ear, Potato Eyes, Potomac Review,* and *The American Indian Culture and Research Journal*. A Windhorse Healing Arts Center board member, O'Haynes conducts workshops on nutrition, journaling to healing, and poetry therapy. At Concord, O'Haynes founded the first Sexual Assault Response Team on a WV state campus. She now uses journaling and poetry therapy to help victims heal. O'Haynes is part Cherokee, teaches Native American Literature and, in addition to the above workshops, conducts seminars on Native American culture and heritage.

Ted Olson teaches Appalachian Studies and English at East Tennessee State University. His books include a collection of poems, *Breathing in*

Darkness (Wind Publications, 2006), and a scholarly study of traditional Appalachian culture, *Blue Ridge Folklife* (University Press of Mississippi, 1998). He is the editor of *CrossRoads: A Southern Culture Annual* (Mercer University Press), and he edited the music section of *The Encyclopedia of Appalachia* (University of Tennessee Press, 2006) and co-edited (with Charles K. Wolfe) *The Bristol Sessions: Writings About the Big Bang of Country Music* (McFarland & Company, Inc., 2005).

Jay Parini was born in Pittston, PA, and went to high school in Scranton. After visiting St. Andrews in Scotland during his undergraduate work, he returned to earn his doctorate from St. Andrews, taught at Dartmouth College, and began teaching at Middlebury College, Vermont, in 1982, where he is the Axinn Professor of English. Although he has published six novels, three biographies (of Frost, Steinbeck, and Faulkner), and edited essential collections of essays about American poetry and literature, Parini's poetry has danced around his life in Pennsylvania coal country, particularly his books *Anthracite Country* (1982) and *Town Life* (1988). His novel, *The Patch Boys* (1986), is about the mining industry, and his most recent novel, *The Apprentice Lover*, is partly set in the Pennsylvania coal country. Parini's most recent publications include a book of essays called *The Art of Teaching* (2005) and *The Art of Subtraction: New and Selected Poems* (2005).

Edwina Pendarvis teaches at Marshall University in Huntington, WV. She was born in eastern Kentucky and spent most of her childhood there and in southern West Virginia. Much of her poetry is about people and places in rural and small-town Appalachia. Her work appears in such journals as *Antietam Review, Appalachian Heritage, Appalachian Journal, Louisville Review, Now & Then Magazine, Wind Magazine* and in anthologies, including *Wild Sweet Notes: Fifty Years of West Virginia Poetry* and *Writing Work: Writers on Working Class Writing. Joy Ride*, a collection of her poems, is featured in *Human Landscapes*, by Bottom Dog Press. Blair Mountain Press published her collection *Like the Mountains of China*. Recently, she and poet Harry Gieg co-authored *Duets*, by Shoestring Press.

Mary Lou Pratt lives in Huntington, West Virginia, where she writes poems, stories, and freelance articles. Pratt heads the Reference Department at the Cabell County Public Library. Her poems have appeared in *Western Poetry, Pivot*, and *The Reading Teacher*, among others, and in the anthology *Wild Sweet Notes II*.

Max Price has had poetry on *Mountain Echoes.com*, and his flash fiction has appeared on *Bewrite.com*. He was published in the *Mountain Echoes: Best of the First Year 2003, 2004* collection, and in *Gambit*. He has a short story in the anthology *Mountain Voices*. Price is a member of the Appalachian Wordsmiths, West Virginia Writers, West Virginia Poetry Society, and Ohio Valley Literary Guild. He and his wife Connie live in Ravenswood, West Virginia.

David Salner worked all over the country—in iron ore mines, foundries, machine shops, and sweat shops—including in West Virginia for many years. His poetry appears in many journals. He received a Puffin Foundation grant to research his third collection, *John Henry's Partner Speaks* (Pudding House, 2006). "There is only one solution to the hazards miners face," he says. "Union rights."

Ken Slone has a poetry collection, *At Home in the Mountains* (2001), and an autobiography, *Mountain Teacher—An Eastern Kentucky Teacher Tells His Story* (2005), featuring stories about teaching nontraditional students, both of which were published by the Jesse Stuart Foundation. *Mountain Teacher* is a contemporary version of *The Thread That Runs So True*, illustrating that the spirit of the one-room school still lives in the community-building done in east Kentucky college classrooms today. It includes the last interviews done with James Still before his death in spring 2001. Slone was recently featured reading poems on the new Kentucky Arts Council-produced CD set titled *More Than Music—A Heritage Driving Tour of Kentucky's Route 23*, narrated by Ricky Skaggs. After earning his graduate degree from Xavier University in Cincinnati, Slone returned to his home county of Johnson, where he lives with his wife Debbie, his daughter Beth, and son Stephen. Ken is professor of English at Big Sandy Community and Technical College, where he received the Great Teacher Award in 1999 for teaching students to take pride in their Appalachian heritage.

Barbara Smith is a freelance writer, editor, and medical ethicist. Smith is professor Emerita of Literature and former Chair of the Division of the Humanities, Alderson-Broaddus College, Philippi, WV. Her most recent books include *Their Name Means Medicine: The Story of the Myers Family* (McClain Print, 2005) and *Demonstrative Pronouns: Poetry by Barbara Smith* (WV Writers, 2006). She is also a sports nut.

Larry Smith lives in Huron, Ohio, and is professor emeritus at Firelands College of Bowling Green State University. He grew up in the industrial foothills of the Appalachians in Mingo Junction, Ohio. Smith is the director of Bottom Dog Press, editor of several poetry and prose anthologies, and is a novelist, memoirist, and poet. His latest book is *A River Remains: Poems* (WordTech Editions, 2006).

Bob Snyder (1937-1995) grew up in St. Marys, WV, on the Ohio River north of Parkersburg. He attended West Virginia University on a General Motors Scholarship and went on to graduate school in Cincinnati, where he began publishing poetry. After serving as director of Antioch College Appalachia in Beckley, West Virginia, he entered Harvard's

Graduate School of Education, where he completed his PhD. In 1977. After Snyder published widely in literary journals, his collection, *We'll See Who's a Peasant,* appeared under the pen name "Billy Greenhorn." At the time of his death, he had completed a second collection, *Milky Way Accent.*

Stephen Spencer teaches American literature and serves as Area Coordinator of Humanities at Wilmington College. Both of his parents were born and raised in eastern Kentucky. Like so many people from Appalachia, they migrated to Southern Ohio with their families to find opportunity. After getting married when very young, Spencer's parents set off on their life adventure, taking their family to live in such exotic places as Guam and Hawaii and traveling all over the world. Every summer Stephen's parents take his son and their other grandchildren to the family reunion in the mountains where they can learn about their roots.

James Still (1906-2001) came to Kentucky in 1932 when he began working as a librarian with Hindman Settlement School. Over the next seventy years, he authored novels, short stories, poetry, children books, and more, including *From the Mountain, From the Valley: New and Collected Poems* (2001), edited by Ted Olson. Still became Kentucky's first poet laureate and won two Guggenheim Fellowships, amongst myriad awards. Besides his writing, which was attuned to the people of Knott County, Kentucky, perhaps his most important gift has been the role of nurturing writers from all over the mountains, many of whom appear in this anthology.

A. E. Stringer is the author of a collection of poems, *Channel Markers* (Wesleyan University Press, 1987)). His work has appeared in such journals as *The Nation, Antaeus, The Ohio Review, Denver Quarterly, The Laurel Review, Shenandoah,* and in two recent anthologies of West Virginia writers, *Wild Sweet Notes* and *Backcountry.* He is a Professor of English at Marshall University.

Jesse Stuart (1906-1984) was born, raised, and lived in Greenup County, Kentucky. During his life time, he published 2,000 poems, 400 short stories, and 60 books. Son of a farmer, Stuart wrote about, was part of, and worked all his life to value the Appalachian culture in northeastern Kentucky. Stuart was inspired by tension between industrialism and his own agrarian way of life. The poem in our anthology is taken from *Songs of a Mountain Plowman,* which was Stuart's second book but was not published until 1986. Late in his life, Stuart established the Jesse Stuart Foundation, which is devoted to Stuart's legacy, W-Hollow, and the Appalachian way of life. Since then, JSF has published over one hundred books and has helped to circulate thousands of titles throughout the region.

John Taylor is the son of a coal miner who had been laid off and migrated to Detroit and the grandson of a coal miner who, in 1916, helped organize the first UMWA local in Monongalia County, West Virginia. In the 1970s Taylor became a lawyer for Chrysler, got fired, went to work at a Chrysler plant, got fired for his work in the safety strikes, and went back to being a lawyer for a labor law firm in Detroit, where he litigated workers' compensation and black lung claims. Taylor went on to become legal counsel for UMWA District 17, the largest district of the union, in Charleston, West Virginia. Taylor now lives in Huntington close to his grandchildren. He then started a private law practice in black lung, workers' compensation, and social security disability. Following his retirement he has been active in the anti-mountaintop removal movement. Taylor now lives in Huntington with his wife, Lynda Ann Ewen, and near to three of his grandchildren.

Cindy Tebo currently resides in Catawissa, Missouri, with her husband and teenage son. Her poetry has most recently appeared in *Amaze: The Cinquain Journal* and *American Tanka*. Her interest in the Appalachian area and the coal-mining industry stems from research and previous travels through Kentucky, Tennessee, and West Virginia. While not directly related to the coal-mining industry, she notes that her mother's roots include the Annapolis and Viburnum region of Missouri, which is in the lead-mining district.

Arline Thorn (1946-2006) was born in West Virginia, where she spent most of her life. She graduated *summa cum laude* from Marshall University in 1967 and earned her doctorate in Comparative Literature at the University of Illinois in 1971. From 1971 until her death, she taught at West Virginia State College/University and chaired the English Department from 1986 to 1994. Her scholarly writings include articles on the Holocaust and three articles in the recently published *West Virginia Encyclopedia*. Her poetry has appeared in regional reviews, in publications from Trillium Press, and in *Wild Sweet Notes: Fifty Years of West Virginia Poetry, 1950-1999*, by Publishers Place.

Jim Webb has a voice widely known in the mountains from his writings, activism, and work at Appalshop's WMMT-FM. Webb is a long-time member and past Coordinator of the Southern Appalachian Writers Cooperative (SAWC). A legendary "swarper" and the World's Greatest Flutophone Player, Webb is the founding publisher and editor of *Pine Mountain Sand & Gravel*. His work has appeared in *Appalachian Journal, Aurora, Reck, The Sandy New Era, Strokes, Red Crow, Mucked* (co-editor), and a chapbook, *Buzzsaws in the Rain* (1999). Webb operates a private campground, Wiley's Last Resort, on top of Pine Mountain, in Letcher County, Kentucky. His book, *Get In, Jesus*, a collection of poetry, essays, and sundries, is forthcoming.

Beth Wellington is a Roanoke, Virginia, based journalist and member of Verbal Events, a poetry collective publishing quarterly and offering workshops and readings since its founding in 1985 by the fellows at Bill Stafford's residency at the Atlantic Center for the Arts. Wellington was selected for a second residency at the Center by Fred Chappell. She has won recognition from the Chester Jones Foundation and attended the Hindman Settlement School's Appalachian Writers' Workshop. Beth is a member of the Southern Appalachian Writers Cooperative (SAWC) and the Appalachian Studies Association. She writes monthly features and analysis for the *New River Free Press* and reviews books for that paper and the *Roanoke Times*. From 1980 to 1997, she served as the founding Executive Director for New River Community Sentencing, Inc. She contributes online to SourceWatch.org, Wikipedia.org and Law Library Resource Exchange (LLRX.com). Beth's blog on culture and politics is The Writing Corner (360.yahoo.com/beth_blog).

Don West (1906-1992) was a radical activist, grassroots poet, folklorist, minister, teacher, and labor organizer who wrote for and to the people around him. West was born and grew up in north Georgia and lived throughout the South until founding the Folk Life Center near Pipestem, West Virginia. He authored thousands of poems, essays, and articles throughout the nation with a focus on Appalachia and the South. His *No Lonesome Road: Selected Prose and Poems* was edited by Jeff Biggers and George Brosi (University of Illinois Press, 2004). A biography by Jim Lorence is due out from the same press in 2007.

Billy Edd Wheeler was born and raised in Boone County, West Virginia. He graduated from Berea College and went on to graduate studies in playwriting at Yale. He has authored more than twenty plays, including the long-running *Hatfields & McCoys* at Beckley, West Virginia. He has published two volumes of poetry and five volumes of humor. His most recent book is a 2005 novel called *Kudzu Covers Manhattan*. Besides poetry, his first love is song writing, and his songs have been recorded by Johnny Cash and June Carter (e.g. "Jackson"), Kenny Rogers, Elvis Presley, and Judy Collins. He and his wife Mary have two children and live in Swannanoa, North Carolina. (www.billyeddwheeler.com)

James Wright (1927-1980) was born and grew up in Martins Ferry, Ohio, and wrote eleven volumes of poetry. Throughout his career, Wright's poems arc back into the landscape of humanity in the industrialized, Appalachian Upper Ohio Valley. "Honey," the poem in our anthology, comes from Wright's final book, *The Journey*, which he completed just before his death. For an excellent essay on Wright's connection to Appalachia see Maggie Anderson's "The River Down Home: James Wright and My Hillbilly Father" in *Ohioana Quarterly* (Spring 2001), reprinted by the Ohio Library Association at (http://www.ohioana.org/features/legacy/jwright.asp)

Margie Moore Wright, a graduate of Crum High School (1987), grew up in the southern coalfields of West Virginia. She is a mother, a wife, and an English major at Marshall University. In rural Wayne County, she observed first-hand the struggles and fears of coal mining families. Her father, grandfather, brother, and husband are and were coal miners. Her testimony, as part of the Appalachian legacy—witnessing the wildcat strike of the seventies and enduring the coal-related deaths of close family, friends and neighbors—has inspired her to write. She is proud of her legacy and has been taught to respect it. Wright says it was through her daddy's eyes that she became familiar with the suffering of a coal miner. It is her great love of the mountains and studies of the past that help her re-live the lives of many through her poetry.

Robert Wrigley teaches at the University of Idaho. **His** recent book is *Earthly Meditations: New and Selected Poems* (Penguin, 2006).

Michael Yarrow received his PhD from Rutgers University, writing a dissertation on Appalachian coal miners' class consciousness based on interviews with miners in West Virginia, eastern Kentucky, and western Virginia during the late 1970s. In following years he conducted more interviews exploring the relationship between class and gender consciousness. He was impressed by the articulate analyses and wonderful stories many miners told and edited some of the interviews into a short-line form as poetry, hoping that the form would induce the reader to pay closer attention to what was being revealed.

photograph by Sandee Lloyd

About the Editor

Chris Green (English) is a professor at Marshall University and works closely with the Appalachian Studies Association.

He is author of *Door to Door* (Pudding House, 2000); he edited *Wind Magazine* from 1998-2003, and is co-editor of *Radicalism in the South Since Reconstruction* (Palgrave-Macmillan, due out 2007). Chris's work as a writer, scholar, teacher, and editor is dedicated to bringing people into conversations about who they are, where they live, and what they care about.